Yosemite Stage Driver

The Life and Times of
George Monroe
and His Family

Yosemite Stage Driver

The Life and Times of George Monroe and His Family

By Tom Bopp

Wawona, California
YosemiteMusic
2023

FRONTISPIECE:

George Monroe, c. 1880 photograph by George Fiske
(Courtesy California Historical Society)

Hardcover ISBN: 979-8-9881620-2-5
Paperback ISBN: 979-8-9881620-0-1
Ebook ISBN: 979-8-9881620-1-8

Set in Palatino Linotype

For my wife, Diane Detrick Bopp

TABLE OF CONTENTS

FOREWORD

Although Tom's book is focused on *George Monroe*, it is actually about the Monroe family from 1794 in Pennsylvania to 1912 in Southern California. Their family movements and experiences supported George through much of his life from the east coast to Mariposa County and Yosemite to the story's end in Southern California. This Black family had brushes with slavery, prejudice, and poverty, yet it held together until after George died in 1886 following an accident. At the same time, George's reputation drew from his driving of the coaches of the Washburn and related livery stables into Yosemite.

Just as Tom has fleshed out the family heritage, he also has related it to the development of the Washburn interests in the roads and hotels from Mariposa to Wawona and Yosemite Valley in which George Monroe played a significant part. There are few accounts of Black people in the Sierra, much less whole families. We are fortunate to have this one.

James B. Snyder
Yosemite National Park Historian from 1988-2005.

INTRODUCTION

The story of George Monroe's ascent to the top of his profession lay hidden for a century, languishing amid that tantalizing, antique fragrance of disregarded city records. The only one who remembered the story was an elderly African American blacksmith named George Millen, left alone in San Diego in 1897. Under questioning by the jury in a coroner's inquest, Millen in his southern, possibly Cajun accent, revealed an epic tale that led from the Antebellum South, through the California Gold Rush and the dawn of Yosemite tourism, to Southern California at the brink of the automobile era. In a few deft sentences, Millen rescued his family's history from being forever lost. He also testified to the triumph and power of self-definition that was achieved by his indomitable sister, Mary Ann Monroe.

Mary's son, George Monroe, had in his short life become a famous stagecoach driver and guide, introducing a stellar cast of international celebrities to Yosemite. Mary's husband, Louis, was a civil rights activist following the Civil War. Together the family established and operated a ranch and farm.

Through the entire arc of her life, Mary asserted her inner strength and intelligence though beset by adversity and tragedy, and endured just long enough, as the reader will learn, that the very nature of her death would result in the preservation of her remarkable story.

Reports of George Monroe's transcendent abilities have filtered down to us through occasional articles, inspiring his placement in the title of this book. But it is crucial to remember that the boldness, drive, and strategic agility displayed by Mary and her brother and husband merit them equal standing with their famous son. This is the story of a determined, talented family emerging triumphant from a systemically oppressive cultural milieu of gender and race bias.

To date, knowledge of George Monroe has come primarily from three sources: press coverage of Ulysses S. Grant's visit to Yosemite in 1879, Monroe's 1886 obituary, and writer Ben C. Truman's reminiscences from 1899 and 1903. This book reaches far beyond those sources with fresh, new research.

Essential to the story is the colorful backdrop of Monroe's career with the Yosemite Stage & Turnpike Company, the complex, fascinating social climate in which the Monroes found themselves, and the local and national historic events that so directly affected their lives. The copious endnotes are provided not only to substantiate the story, but to enrich it with extra details, and to provide clues to aid further research.

As a note to the reader from the author's perspective, a history book always becomes more vivid by conjuring up in the imagination the places, the smells, sounds, and feel of the air, and especially the people—the cadence of their voices, and what they might say over dinner if you could only join them.

PREFACE

George Monroe worked as a stage driver for the Washburn brothers and their associates, who created and operated the Yosemite Stage & Turnpike Company and the Wawona Hotel Company. John Washburn was the last surviving of the brothers. After John died in 1917, his son Clarence Washburn headed the two corporations until he liquidated the Y.S.&T.C. and transferred the hotel business to the Yosemite Park & Curry Company, and the company's property holdings to the United States government, in 1932. Clarence's daughter, Wawona Washburn Hartwig (1914-2000) spent an enormous part of her later years researching her family's rich history.

My employment as a musician and entertainer at the Wawona Hotel began in 1983 and brought me into contact with Mrs. Hartwig in the late '80s. In 1989 she asked me to photograph her 75th birthday celebration at the hotel, at which time we formed a close bond that carried through the last decade of her life. Through my friendship with her and shared interest in Wawona's history (both the person and the place), I was asked by the executor of her estate to carry on her work.

Taking the responsibility seriously, and with ever-growing respect for what she'd achieved, in 2001 I began to copy and index all of her research. I also went about indexing several published books covering history related to Wawona and Yosemite. Noting the paucity of source attributions in the published materials, I sought to find the primary sources that had been omitted, first by looking for corroboration of specific events that may have been covered in the *Mariposa Gazette* newspaper microfilm archives in the Yosemite Research Library. In some cases, I found corroboration, but it quickly became apparent that the primary sources often contradicted the history books, and beyond that, there was a wealth of additional information yet to be unearthed.

Over the next five years, I poured through every page of microfilm of the *Gazette* from 1854 to 1901, copying and indexing as much as I could find relating directly or indirectly to Wawona history. Before reaching the 1890s, I began to recognize names that I had not indexed from earlier years—names that had not become significant until later years. While my memory was still fresh, I started over at 1854 to index the names and events that I now knew belonged in the historical stream. After the *Gazette* project, there were several other archives yet to be indexed, many of which I've completed, but with still more to do. With the advent of online digital archiving of newspapers, I've learned that, so far, digital search functions fail to turn up key words and names nearly as well as the more painstaking visual scan with one's own eyes.

A search of my index for George Monroe revealed just about enough material to construct a biography or at least a chapter in a larger book. Among the indexed items was a notice in the *Gazette* about the death of Mary Monroe, George's mother, in San Diego in 1897. This led to a visit to the San Diego History Center Research Archives, where I was provided with a copy of Mary Monroe's Coroner's Inquest, and two related stories in the *San Diego Union* newspaper. This new data, combined with my previous research, was enough to bring the Monroes' extraordinary saga to life.

To give as accurately as possible a feel for the life and times of George Monroe, a good deal of text from primary sources is provided, as in an anthology. While some historical source-material about Monroe is known to exist in private collections, I have focused my research on sources that are freely available to serious researchers, so that it may be checked for accuracy and expanded upon as more documents become public.

YOSEMITE STAGE AND TURNPIKE CO.

"Just as there are the greatest of soldiers and sailors, artists and mechanics at times, so there are greater stage drivers than their fellows and George Monroe was the greatest of all."

– Albert Henry Washburn, Superintendent,
  Yosemite Stage & Turnpike Co.

Chapter I

Saturday evening, the twenty-seventh of November 1897, Mariposa, California—More than a few old timers shaking open the *Mariposa Gazette* were likely jolted into remembrance of their old neighbor, Mary Monroe. Here was an unfitting end for someone of her achievements, an African-American woman who had left her home in antebellum Georgia, journeyed alone into the unruly chaos of the California Gold Rush to rescue her husband from an unseemly fate, and to top it all raised their son to become the most celebrated stage driver at the dawn of Yosemite tourism.

Before catching the sad little blurb about Mary, readers would first have scanned the local items: James McCauley stripped of control of his hotel at Glacier Point in Yosemite. John Tatum convicted of a Yosemite stage holdup. An advertisement proclaiming, "Don't go to Klondike without taking along a Winchester Repeating Rifle." And then:

> "Mrs. Mary A. Monroe, an aged colored lady, who formerly lived in Mariposa but recently a resident of San Diego, was killed by an electric car in that city on the 14th of this month. Mrs. Monroe was deaf and stepped directly in front of the approaching car without noticing it. —Merced Star"[1]

Pausing over the news, older readers of the *Gazette* might have pictured the Monroes on their ranch down at Pea Ridge. Their place was easy enough to find—just head south from town along Mariposa Creek through Mormon Bar, then loop southeast around the bulge of Lookout Mountain. It's all typically beautiful Sierra foothill scenery with plenty of grass, peppered with oaks, pines, manzanita, and the like. A rough, narrow, rocky wagon road wound through the hills, affording glimpses of Red Mountain and the lower Sierra Nevada mountains, dipping along creeks in cool shaded glens. About six miles from Mariposa you'd arrive at Pea Ridge, also called the Red Mountain or Chowchilla district, in reference to the Chowchilla River (west fork) and Red Mountain, both within four miles to the east.

With the setting sun and a sliver of moon outside the window on that cool Saturday evening, long-time residents folding their newspapers surely felt the passing of an extraordinary family— their neighbors for over 35 years.[2]

Road skirting Monroe Ranch site (Author photograph)[3]

Mary's labors in building the family ranch were admired throughout the district. Her husband had been a well-known barber in Mariposa and a pillar of the local Black community. A few might have remembered Mary's brother, George Millen, a blacksmith who had lived and worked for a few years at Pea Ridge. But Mary's son, George, had become a legend. His portrait graces the lobby of the Wawona Hotel, where he picked up and delivered countless travelers. Today, guests looking into Monroe's quiet eyes are given to wonder what stories they might tell.

West-southwest view of Washington, D.C. from the Capitol, c. 1863
Includes The Mall, Smithsonian Castle, Washington Canal, Botanic Garden,
Washington Monument under construction, and the Potomac River
(Library of Congress Prints and Photographs Division)

(Detail from above photograph)

THE MILLENS—*George Monroe's mother; Pennsylvania to Georgia.*

Forty-three years before that fateful *Gazette* article, the year of 1854 would find the seven-year-old George Monroe in a Washington D.C. school, grappling with arithmetic, learning Bible stories and memorizing verses, building his vocabulary, and trying to write in a round, legible hand. The improbability that George or any other Black child would be sitting in a classroom at that time is staggering, but it is also completely in line with the unlikely circumstances that had brought him there in the first place.

Leaning into the arithmetic quiz on his desk, George might have felt on his young shoulders the considerable weight of his family's legacy. Perhaps that's what lent to the quiet, pensive nature ascribed to him in later years. Those later descriptions also indicate that he was perceptive, attentive, and likely possessed the gentle empathy that would accompany his affinity with horses. He had a dry sense of humor, and he also had a penchant for nice clothes, probably inherited from his maternal grandfather who had been a tailor. Young George was also described as "civil, polite, studious and industrious."[4]

This smart, sensitive, nicely-dressed kid would need to concentrate and focus, filtering out thoughts of his highly distracting circumstances. School must have seemed illicit, even frightening, for a child from Georgia where it was illegal to teach Black kids to read. Now here he was in a strange city, living with his uncle George and trying to take a math test, possibly wondering if he would ever see his mother and father again.

It was a bit much for a seven-year-old to absorb. Two years earlier, his father and uncle had left their home in Georgia for the gold-fields of California. Then just recently his uncle had returned home—alone—having left George's father back in California for reasons that the boy was just too young to understand. Now all of a sudden young George was uprooted from his childhood home by his mother and uncle, bidding his grandmother Polly a tearful goodbye as they whisked away on the train to New York City. Standing on the dock with his uncle, the disoriented little boy would wave to his mother as she sailed alone out of New York harbor on a steamer bound for California. The two Georges, Millen and Monroe—a resolute uncle and his bewildered nephew—then traveled south to take up residence together in the nation's capital. Years would have to pass before young George could be told the story of what had led to his present circumstances.

Once settled in Washington, D.C., George Millen probably found work as a blacksmith, most likely in the southwest section of the city which was populated by other free African Americans. This section would have attracted Millen for one very specific reason: it was here that Rev. Anthony Bowen had a school for free Black children, and had the previous year established the very first African American chapter of the YMCA. From this section of the city, residents could see and hear nearby workers building, stone by stone, what would become the Washington Monument. Competing for attention was another nearby construction project called The Castle, the future home of the Smithsonian Institution.[5]

The two Georges most likely stayed in a boarding house, funded by Millen's income and perhaps supplemented by his sister, Mary. Young George would walk to school while his uncle walked to a local blacksmith shop. After school, George might head to his uncle's workplace, where he could find solace among the horses—far more companionable than stern adults and noisy schoolmates.

All George Monroe could have known for sure was that his uncle and mother were taking pains on his behalf and had sacrificed greatly to put him in school, and that he had better apply himself to his studies. From his boy's perspective, he may have reasoned that if he did well in school, his parents would come back home or, even better, send for him and Uncle George to join them in California.

It is hard to guess how much the family might have shared with young George. As he was only about five when his father left home, he may not have heard his father's story, if it ever really happened, of being freed from slavery and taken by British soldiers from Maryland to Nova Scotia, then later sailing back to Georgia. His mother certainly had stories to tell about her childhood, and how she cared for her little brother—George's uncle—when he was a baby. Young George might also have heard his uncle's stories about California and Mexico, and what it was like growing up in an adoptive French family. If George sensed that his uncle and parents seemed a bit exotic, compared to the other kids' adult relatives, it was not without good cause. And though he wasn't old enough to know the whole truth of his present situation, his uncle certainly did.

George Millen unveiled that story forty-three years later, two days after Mary's death. He had been called to testify at a coroner's inquest into the death of his sister, chiefly to identify Mary's remains and establish the validity of his relationship to her, but during the inquiry, he would also relate some fascinating history. In a remarkably compact statement, George Millen left us just enough clues to reveal how George Monroe happened to be a free African American, in school, years before the Emancipation Proclamation, and why he was living with his uncle while his parents were so very far away. Millen's casual references to Mexico, to living with a French family, and trekking to the California gold fields with Mary's husband, begin to show that George Monroe belonged to an extraordinary family.

THE CORONER'S INQUEST—*George Millen reveals the family history.*

The last surviving and youngest of Mary's five siblings, George Millen was undergoing questioning by the City of San Diego Coroner's Inquest into the death of Mary Monroe. It was a Tuesday, the sixteenth of November 1897, just two days after her accident; her broken body lay in Johnson's Undertaking Parlors after having been examined by the coroner, Dr. Theodore F. Johnson, and ten jurors. After a good deal of testimony by witnesses to the accident and acquaintances of the deceased, Millen was sworn in and proceeded to outline his family's history. He'd worked as a blacksmith in San Diego for ten years, and had persuaded Mary to join him there:[6]

"Soon after the death of her husband she written me and I written her too, that she better come here and live with me. Later she [wrote] to me from Frisco [San Francisco] when she was coming and I got rooms at Mrs. Bell's and she remained there until she broke up and went with some family. She never knew what it was to work for families or anybody else until she came to [San Diego]."[7]

George Millen gave his birth as August 1825, and then proceeded with a sketch of his family history:[8]

"[Mary cared for] me when I was a little boy and she was a good big girl. There was one [sibling] between me and her. My father lived in what was called Westbury; he was a tailor by profession, and there he lived, and he was taken sick and he moved to Augusta, Georgia, and there he died when I was a small boy, and I was raised by a French family. I lived in the

8

same town [as Mary] until later years, she moved out to Columbus, Georgia, from Augusta, Georgia. My mother died about '67 or '68, I think, I do not remember now, I cannot say accurately."

Millen's suggestion that Mary was older didn't jibe with the official information, so the coroner pursued the question:

"Q. How old was she?
A. She ought to be about seventy-five.
Q. She was older than you?
A. Yes sir. They have got her age down much less, but she was older than me. I do not deny anything, and there is a great many people don't like their age to be known but if I was a hundred and fifty I should make it known very readily."

Millen's estimate puts Mary at three years older than him, with a birth year of 1822.[9]

George Millen's statement to the coroner, combined with the few remaining census records, allows the construction of a hypothetical scenario for the Millen family's history:

George and Mary Millen's parents, Polly and George Sr., born near the turn of the 19th century in Pennsylvania, moved to Waynesboro, just south of Augusta, Georgia by 1820. After two years, 1822 finds the Millen family in Ohio where Mary is born. From Ohio they move to Westbury, Pennsylvania, where the father is taken with a sudden grave illness, perhaps initiating their abrupt return to Waynesboro by 1825 where George (junior) is born.[10]

```
1  In the Matter of the              )
2  Coroner's Inquest over the        )
3  Body of Mary A. Munroe, Deceased. )
4  Held before Theo. F. Johnson,     )
5  Coroner, at Johnson's Undertaking )
6  Parlors.                          )

7
8                    San Diego, Cal. Tuesday, Nov. 16, 1897.
9        W. W. Whitson is appointed by the Coroner to report the
10  testimony and proceedings herein in shorthand, and directed
11  to transcribe the same.
12        The following named persons were selected and sworn as
13  jurors, namely:
14        Charles W. Averill, F. H. Rediger, C. Holmquist, Sam
15  Sprecher, J. H. Hopper, George McIntyre, J. F. Neeley, E. A.
16  Stevens, N. S. Low, and L. Weiland.
17        THE CORONER: We have ten jurors, we will proceed.
18  Now if you will, just come this way and view the body.
19        Jurors view the body.
```

Coroner's Inquest, first page (San Diego History Center)

George and Mary's father appears to be George Millen, Sr., and their mother was Polly Millen. Thirty miles south of Augusta in Waynesboro, the 1820 census describes a household of "Free Colored Persons" headed by a "George Millin [sic]," including one male and female under age 14, another female aged between 14-25 years old (consistent with Polly's age of 20), and a male aged between 26-44 years old (probably George, Sr.). Also, there is listed one enslaved female in the household, possibly a family member who had been purchased and freed by Millen, with the transaction yet to be officially documented (this practice accounts for many cases that give the false appearance of African Americans enslaving other people).[11]

It has not come to light how it was that Polly and George Millen, Sr. were free. George Jr.'s description of his father as a "tailor by profession" indicates he was not enslaved but worked for wages, and that his children were free-born.

In the years between the American Revolution and the close of the eighteenth century, the international slave trade was banned in all the states except Georgia and South Carolina. Though many held fast to the institution of slavery, in many states thousands of enslaved people were freed during this time. Additionally, enslaved people could sometimes achieve freedom through various other means, including escape, or by self-purchase. For example, as sometimes allowed by their enslavers, enslaved people could produce and save income by selling services or products created during the evening hours and on Sundays, including the sale of produce from their own gardens, eventually raising enough to purchase their freedom.[12]

Mary recorded that her parents were born in Pennsylvania, where slavery had been outlawed in 1780 and Quakers and others were actively involved with abolition. By 1820, the Millens had moved to Waynesboro, Georgia. So far, one can only speculate as to why they would choose to move from the relative sanctuary of Pennsylvania to the slavery-state of Georgia—perhaps family members lived there. But two years later finds the Millen family in Ohio, in time for Mary's birth in 1822. It isn't surprising that a move to Ohio would have been an attractive prospect. In Ohio, slavery had been prohibited since the Northwest Ordinance of 1787, and there was considerable activity with the Underground Railroad. Ohio also offered educational opportunities for African

Americans, where ten years later Oberlin College would offer them higher education.[13]

Coincidentally near the same presumed time and place of Mary's birth, a family in Point Pleasant, Ohio was celebrating the birth of a son in April 1822: Hiram Ulysses Grant (who would later change his name to Ulysses S. Grant).

Separated by a stretch of rolling Ohio countryside, the infant boy and girl lay in their cots, linked on a trajectory that would eventually bring them both together, but only after the passage of five tumultuous decades. Having been born a White male, the baby Grant would enjoy a spectrum of privileges that Mary, as a Black female, would be denied. In their respective ways, Mary and Ulysses would confront the injustice as a common challenge — Grant, through war and legislation, and Mary, with bold strategic actions to preserve her family.

One of Mary's strategies would be to diligently monitor Grant's achievements toward racial equality and apply them to the success of her family. Thus, the two newborns would come to share triumphs over the very inequities that stood between them, directing their futures toward an unlikely convergence. That convergence wouldn't happen for another fifty-seven years, when Grant would join Mary's son for two extraordinary days in a place, as yet unknown to them, that would be called Yosemite.

Sometime before 1825, the Millens would move their family from Ohio and return to Pennsylvania. George Jr. had heard growing up that his father (and presumably the rest of his family) lived in "what was called Westbury." This probably refers to Westbury, Moreland Township, Pennsylvania. Westbury lies on the Old York Road, which linked the Underground Railroad from Philadelphia and Willow Grove (3 miles south of Westbury) to New York. Estimates put the African American population of Moreland Township in the year 1776 at 100, about 25 of whom may have been enslaved.[14]

According to George Jr.'s later testimony, his father became ill enough to prompt an abrupt departure from Westbury and a return of the family to Georgia, in time for George Jr. to be born there in 1825. In an indication that George Sr. continued to suffer from a chronic medical condition, his wife Polly was evidently so overworked that she delegated their daughter Mary, just a child herself, to care for her little brother.

The 1830 census finds the Millen household still living in Waynesboro, with the approximate ages of the two oldest household members consistent with those of George Sr. and Polly. But in 1834, a Waynesboro newspaper reported that Polly had not been picking up her mail at the Post Office. The fact that Polly was named in the article and not her husband, along with the neglected stack of accumulated mail, leaves a poignant suggestion that her husband may have died at about that time.[15]

Twelve-year-old Mary Millen would have had to grow up quickly. So very young when her father died, having already lived in three different states, Mary's childhood must have seemed to her a bewildering odyssey. But through it all, her determined and hard-working mother, Polly Millen, carried the family forward, just as Mary would in the coming years. Faced with the daunting responsibility of supporting six children as a single mother, Polly moved her family thirty miles north to Augusta.

Situated on the Savannah River, Augusta was a busy trade center (including the slave trade), and the robust economy would have offered greater work opportunities, not only for Polly but for her children. The 1840 Census shows forty-year-old Polly Millen as the head of the household, a family of seven "Free Colored Persons." By that time her family included 3 males and one female aged between 10 and 23, and two girls less than 10 years of age.

In another indication of the stress her family was facing, Polly allowed her youngest child, George, to be adopted by a nearby French family. It is probably during this time that George learned the trade of blacksmithing. George Millen's adoptive family would have been related to one of several distinct groups of French immigrants to Georgia. These included descendants of refugees from the French Revolution, and the Huguenots—Calvinists who had fled religious persecution under Louis XIV. Also, there were French colonists who in the 1790s escaped the Haitian slave rebellions, and the Acadians—French Catholics ousted from Nova Scotia by the British in the mid-1700s. Two of these groups stand out as the most likely candidates for George Millen's new family. In Georgia, descendants of the Huguenots often affiliated themselves with the Anglican Church which opposed slavery, and their descendants may have been agreeable to adopting George. The other possibility, that he lived with a family of Acadians, leads to an intriguing theory that links the Millen and Monroe families and sets the stage for the marriage of Louis Monroe and Mary Millen.[16]

THE MONROES—*An intriguing theory about Louis Monroe escaping enslavement to a British colony in Nova Scotia. Mary Millen and Louis Monroe wed.*

Though seven-year-old George Monroe surely remembered his father, his memories would have been the childlike images and vignettes formed during the first five years of his life. Over the next two years after his father left for California, George probably formed an extra bond with his mother, Mary, in much the same way that Mary would have with her mother, Polly. Now young George was likely getting to know his uncle pretty well while his mother was gone, but he probably had little more than an inkling of his father's dramatic backstory, if the story is true. The story is indeed true in that it truly happened—to somebody—but whether it happened to George Monroe's father Louis raises a compelling theory. The theory goes like this:

> In 1814, young Louis Monroe and his family, enslaved on a Maryland farm, are freed in a raid by the British Navy. They are then shipped to a colony in Nova Scotia where, with other freed former slaves, they try to eke out a living farming land licensed to them by the British. After some years of toil and extreme winters, Louis and some of his family, along with other disillusioned immigrants, take advantage of British offers to transport them south, out of the country.
>
> Some of the Monroe family decide to return to Georgia, perhaps because they had lived there before their enslavement in Maryland. With assurances from British officials and their French-Acadian neighbors in Nova Scotia, the Monroes are willing to take the chance that they will be insulated and protected in Georgia, living within a colony of sympathetic, anti-slavery Acadians who had been similarly removed from Nova Scotia. In Georgia, Louis grows to manhood among French-Acadian families near Augusta, including one French family that has adopted the brother of his future wife, Mary Millen.

Here is the improbable backstory that ties this theory together.

In the 1600s, French colonists established themselves in Nova Scotia as the first European settlers of a land they called Acadia. The Acadians clung to their independence even after their province became British in 1713. Friction created by the Acadians' refusal to join the British military led to the so-called Expulsion of The Acadians, when the British forcibly deported thousands of Acadians to the American colonies in the mid-1700s. In the years after the expulsion, however, many Acadian families returned home and by 1800 were once again well-established in Nova Scotia.

About two years into the War of 1812, the British offered American deserters—including enslaved people—the right to free settlement in British colonies. Under this arrangement, an estimated 2,000 newly-freed people, known to historians as the Black Refugees, were transported from the United States to freedom in Nova Scotia by 1816. Two of the Black Refugees bore the name Lewis Munroe.[17]

Enslaved workers' quarters at Sotterley Plantation[18]
(Library of Congress)

In September 1814, the British fleet was advancing up the Patuxent River into Maryland. John R. Plater probably watched with considerable anxiety as an enemy frigate, the forty-gun *HMS Severn*, pulled up and anchored abreast of his beloved Sotterley

Plantation. Plater was put in charge of Sotterley until his young nephew, heir to the estate when Plater's brother died, reached manhood and could manage the thousands of acres of tobacco, grains, livestock, and dozens of enslaved people.

Plater was surely helpless to resist while British soldiers spilled over the deck, rowed ashore, and proceeded to burn all of his crops. During the assault, the ship's captain and a few of the soldiers, as Plater later described it, "seduced and carried away" about forty enslaved people. These forty men, women, and children were suddenly faced with a spur-of-the-moment decision, solely based upon the word of men who were busily destroying their oppressor's farm. They could either remain in bondage and work to replant Plater's ravaged fields, or they could board a ship filled with soldiers and journey to an unknown destination where they may or may not receive land and freedom as offered by the captain. That Plater said that they were "seduced" indicates that they were not taken by force, but had instead chosen to risk an uncertain future that offered freedom, rather than to remain enslaved at Sotterley.

These newly liberated people would soon join hundreds of other Black Refugees for transportation to the north. Three of those formerly enslaved by Plater, including one named Lewis Munroe, were assigned land on Halifax Harbor, Nova Scotia.[19]

Plater later filed a claim with county officials, seeking reparations for losses regarding the people who'd been liberated from his bondage. Affixing monetary values to each enslaved man, woman, and child, he listed them all by name and age, including these seven with the last name of Munroe:

Lewis, house servant, age 26, $600
Grace, cook, age 27, $400
Gerard, age 14, $500
Ester, age 7, $150

17

Richard, age 5, $225

Lewis, age 3, $150

Kitty, age 2, $100[20]

Records from 1815 and 1816 describe the Munroe family as having "settled upon lands conveyed to them by Henry H. Cogswell which lands are dedicated at the Head of the North West Arm [of Halifax Harbor, Nova Scotia]."

The Munroes and their fellow Black Refugees were now faced with adapting to a new land and climate. Some of the refugees had died during the rough autumn sea journey from the southern coast, and others would die from exposure in the coming winters. The Munroes' neighbors included two other refugee families from Sotterley, Stephen Coursey with his wife and four children, and Benjamin Seale with his family of ten, all given licenses to occupy farmlands owned by Henry Cogswell on Halifax Harbor. They would all be dependent upon their benefactors for food and shelter until they could establish some means of sustaining themselves. On Christmas Eve 1815, Cogswell wrote to the local governor that families on his land had only the clothing they'd brought from Maryland.[21]

Conditions were made even worse for the refugees by a post-war depression, but the British government and landlords like Cogswell still held responsibility for their welfare. Though the locals were generally opposed to slavery, their unease with the presence of the Black Refugees likely contributed to an effort by governmental authorities to devise various schemes to encourage them to leave. Despite the difficult environment, most of the refugees remained in the area, but not all. In 1821, 95 of the Black Refugees were persuaded by an offer from Lieutenant Governor Lord Dalhousie to transport them all to Trinidad.

To play out in the mind's eye the improbable odyssey of those 95 Black Refugees challenges the imagination. They, or their

18

ancestors, were taken from Africa, enslaved in America, carried by British soldiers from Maryland to freedom in Nova Scotia, then seven years later transported south to Trinidad. It is possible that young Louis Monroe endured a similar path, with the exception that Louis, rather than sailing to Trinidad, would instead travel to Georgia.

The migratory history of the Acadians and Black Refugees between Nova Scotia and the American South supports the possibility that the younger *Lewis Munroe* in John Plater's list of enslaved people could be the *Louis Monroe* who later became Mary Millen's husband. Additional support comes from Plater's record of the birth-year for the younger Lewis Munroe as 1811, only six years off from the birth-year of 1817 given for *Louis Monroe* in the 1850 federal census. Freed formerly enslaved people were a rarity, and written documentation of their names even more so. Within this narrow range of surviving records, the apparent improbability of finding three references to African Americans with the same name—Lewis Munroe the elder and younger, and Louis Monroe of Augusta, Georgia—suggests that they may be connected.[22]

George Millen's adoptive French family were probably Acadians, or Cajuns as they are known in the United States, and probably would have stayed in touch with their friends and relatives left behind in Halifax, Nova Scotia. With a shared experience of oppression in Nova Scotia, along with their opposition to slavery, the Cajuns and the Black Refugees had more than a little in common. Perhaps the Monroes, having befriended their Acadian neighbors in Halifax, learned that there were sympathetic Cajuns down in Augusta, Georgia, ready to welcome a family of free Black Refugees.

All that is truly known is this: In the 1840s, Mary Millen lived with her family of free African Americans in a neighborhood near Augusta, Georgia. Within her circle was a French family that adopted Mary's brother, George. Mary fell in love with a local barber named Louis Monroe, they married and had a son who would become the subject of this book. What is also known is the incredible story of Lewis Munroe from Sotterley Plantation. Whether Monroe the barber is one and the same as Munroe from Sotterley, remains unconfirmed.[23]

George Millen recalled that Mary had left Augusta "in later years," moving some 200 miles southwest to Columbus, Georgia, a major manufacturing center at the time. Still single and in her mid-twenties, Mary appears to have continued to live with her mother and remaining siblings. Rather than seeking outside employment, she may have worked to sustain the family by raising farm products for themselves and to sell. As noted later in her brother's testimony from 1897: "[Mary] never knew what it was to work for families or anybody else."

Louis Augustus Monroe and Mary A. Millen were married by 1847, which was also the birth year of their son, George Frazier Monroe. It remains to be discovered whether the marriage and birth of their son took place before or after Mary's move from Augusta, but by 1850 the census shows Louis, Mary, and young George living together with Mary's mother, Polly, in Columbus, Georgia. At some point, according to George Millen, Mary had given birth to another child. The wording of her brother's testimony faintly suggests that the child may have been their son's twin sibling—when asked if Mary had any children, George had answered, "One child, sir—had two, but one lived and the other died."[24]

The 1850 census suggests that Mary had two younger brothers also living in Columbus, both listed as "M" for "Mulatto." James Millen, aged twenty-two, worked for William Switzer who owned a hotel in conjunction with a mill—possibly a cotton mill. Living close to Mary (as indicated by their adjacent entries in the census) was David Millen, aged twenty-four, his wife Priscilla, and their two young sons John, aged two, and David Jr. aged six months.[25]

James and David Millen had something in common with Mary's husband—all three men were employed in the practical and portable trade of barbering. Free African Americans, though impeded by discriminatory laws, participated in society as property owners and professionals in a wide range of vocations, particularly when they fell within the acceptable norms of White clients, as with barbering. A notable example, some 400 miles to the west of Columbus, in Natchez, Mississippi, was an African American barber named William Tiler Johnson. Born into enslavement in 1809 and freed in 1820, Johnson owned land, enslaved people, loaned money and ran a successful barber shop in the 1830s and '40s. A window into the often brutal culture of that time and place, Johnson's own diary describes his whipping of his enslaved laborers to instill discipline.[26]

George Millen was now in his early twenties. A self-described rover, George recalled in his 1897 testimony:

> "I have been a mover, always a resident wherever I stopped, but I have never stayed no place because I have never been satisfied in the United States. … I left Georgia and went to Mexico in forty-six or seven. I then went back to Georgia and I then came to California in '52 …."

Millen's departure for Mexico at that time may have coincided with the migration to Columbus of his mother and sister. It also coincided with the outbreak of the Mexican War (also called the Mexican-American War), but it is not apparent whether he participated in it. Mexico had abolished slavery in 1837, including in the province that would become Texas, but the U.S. annexation of Texas, and the ensuing war, promised to convert the area into a slavery state. Some African Americans served on U.S. Navy ships during the war and others in the U.S. Army, most commonly as enslaved servants of White officers and soldiers.

Ulysses S. Grant, though stating that he was "bitterly opposed" to the action, served as an officer in that war. Before and during the conflict a sizable number of people escaped slavery into Mexico to gain their freedom. Some of the escapees found a warm welcome there, while many others were compelled by harsh circumstances to return to the United States. Millen, a free African American like his sister, may have sought to personally investigate whether Mexico offered a more welcoming environment. He may even have gone to join friends or relatives who'd escaped over the border and possibly enlisted in the Mexican army. Whatever the case, Millen returned to Georgia by 1852 and resumed contact with his sister and family in Columbus.[27]

LEAVING GEORGIA—*George Monroe's father, uncle, and later his mother, join the Gold Rush to California, while George attends school in Washington, D.C., after which they reunite with Louis and Mary in California.*

Though their freedom was upheld by law and documented by their "free papers," free African Americans were, in the words of one historian, "the object of unceasing interest, suspicion and often hostility in a land where Negroes were generally considered a race of slaves to be insulated from all aspirations to freedom." The surrounding culture of institutionalized enslavement could only have been a continuing source of stress, and the possibility of moving away to a less hostile land a constant, nagging enticement.[28]

George Monroe's family may have had a different, broader perspective than many of their neighbors. George's grandparents and his mother had lived in free northern states; his father may have been as far as Nova Scotia, and now his uncle had ventured to Mexico. They all had their free papers and the literacy that enabled them to learn about the outside world. Faced with the responsibility for their child's future, George Monroe's family may have assessed his prospects for a good life in Columbus as fairly bleak.

Casting their imaginations more broadly, the family dinner conversations evidently turned increasingly to current news of the burgeoning economy in a new state called California, where the constitution outlawed slavery. It might be too much of a gamble for the entire family to pull up stakes and head west, so a more conservative scheme would be devised to send a scouting expedition. So it was that in 1852 when George was five years old, the possibilities for his future took a decisive turn. That year, remaining at home with his mother and grandmother, George would wave goodbye to his father and uncle George as they left Columbus to join the California Gold Rush. This was not a lark; it was a mission.

Such a venture might at least produce income to send home, but more importantly, it could lead to a family exodus from Georgia to a better life, and a better future for young George. While his uncle's foray into Mexico may have failed to raise any prospects for a family emigration, California's economic prosperity would certainly provide opportunities for Louis as a barber and George as a blacksmith. Whether it would provide a suitable home for the family remained to be seen. Either way, it would be an adventure for Louis and his brother-in-law. It could take over three weeks to reach San Francisco, and possibly two or more days by stagecoach to reach the gold fields. In packing for the trip, Louis would have included his barbering tools, but he was in his prime, and panning for gold might just suit him, too.

By a striking coincidence, July of that same year found Ulysses S. Grant making the same trip to California, packing over seven hundred soldiers of the 4th Infantry along with gold-seekers and others onto the aging steamship *Ohio*. Born near the same time and place as Mary Millen, soldiering in Mexico when George Millen was also there, and now en route to California in tandem with Mary's husband and brother, it almost seems as though Grant was shadowing her family.[29]

Auburn Ravine, 1852, attributed to Joseph B. Starkweather (Courtesy of the California History Room, California State Library)

Through the year of 1852 and well into the next, George and Louis were immersed in a climate and culture that was entirely foreign to them. The camps and gold fields were crowded with a stimulating diversity of adventurous men, often segregated into places with names like Italian Bar, Chinese Camp, Spanish Flat, Negro Butte, and far to the south, Arroyo de los Negros. Considering their options, it seems most likely that the two brothers-in-law would have decided to set up shop as blacksmith and barber, though they certainly had the choice to pursue work as laborers.[30]

Over the next year or so, having endured the seasonal challenges of snowy winters and searing summers, the two argonauts appear to have earned enough money to engage in some discretionary spending. George would have kept his eye on the family goal to find them a place to settle in California and may have made inquiries about hospitable areas in which the Monroes could begin a new life. While there was certainly racism in the wild west, the robust economy and the outlawing of slavery in the state may have looked encouraging, and George would surely have been paying attention to travelers' stories about the social climates in various towns around California. Louis, on the other hand, seemed to be losing his grip on things and forgetting the reason he was there.

After less than two years working alongside his brother-in-law and adapting (or not) to life in the bawdy gold camps of Calaveras County, George Millen was becoming increasingly disturbed about Louis' behavior. Though he left no details about his brother-in-law's indiscretions, George's reaction to them indicates their seriousness. Instead of working toward a better future for his family, Louis was somehow jeopardizing the entire venture so badly that Millen was compelled to walk out on his own brother-in-law.

George likely had some sharp parting words with Louis before taking his leave. Then, instead of relocating to some other town, George turned his back on the gold camps, headed down to San Francisco, booked passage for the long journey to the east coast, and returned to his sister and nephew in Georgia. His fateful and selfless decision set into motion a chain of events that rocked the entire family and brought about a hasty exit from their Georgia home. George Millen told the story:

"Myself and [Mary's] husband and three or four young men came to Calaveras County in 1852. I found that her husband was getting reckless and I went back east and apprised her of the change and had her sell her property and I took her on to New York and let her come to California. It must have been the first of '54."

What "reckless" may mean isn't hard to imagine in the context of the many descriptions of life in the gold camps. As long as one had money and the inclination—and Louis apparently had enough of both—there were plenty of opportunities for recklessness in the ubiquitous saloons and gambling halls. Millen put it simply, "He, like most young men, got reckless when he got [to California]."[31]

When George Millen arrived back in Columbus, Georgia, the reunion at his sister's home was probably a bit subdued and anxious. George had the awkward duty to apprise Mary of her husband's activities. Beyond that, George would have described what he'd seen regarding the attributes of California as a destination for the family. Mary's mother, Polly, no doubt had more than a few sharp words to express about her son-in-law, and about what might become of her grandson, George. Taking it all in, Mary must have been troubled, if not outright alarmed, that her husband was threatening her family's chance to move west, and she decided it was time to act.

Through it all, George Millen's devotion to his sister merits considerable respect. She had helped raise him when they were children, which may have lent to a special bond between the siblings. For him to leave the promise and excitement of the gold fields to make the lengthy and expensive trip back to Georgia was no small thing. Beyond that, for his sister to then sell her belongings and take the same journey—by herself—into that wild exotic land in search of her husband is just extraordinary. At least she had her loyal brother to give travel advice, and to remain with her seven-year-old son while she ventured west to salvage her marriage.

And that is the story of how young George Monroe had found himself in a boarding house, living with his uncle in Washington, D.C., seven-hundred miles from his former home, attending school. His mother had sold her property and was by now some twenty-five-hundred miles to the west looking for his father, while George did his best to keep up with his schoolwork.

It was nine long years before the Emancipation Proclamation. This son of free African Americans was experiencing the beginning of what would continue to be an extraordinary life. There can be no doubt of the high value his family placed on education. Locating a school, packing up and moving far away, finding a new residence, and getting young George enrolled required deliberate effort, planning, and resourcefulness. Multiple census records confirm that George and his parents had learned to read and write, despite Georgia law that made it a misdemeanor to teach literacy to either free or enslaved African Americans.[32]

George's mother and uncle had threaded him through the statistical eye of a needle. Of the recorded 17,069,453 souls counted by the 1850 United States Census, 16.1% were recorded as Black, and of them, about 14% (386,293) were free African Americans. Where the Millen family had lived in Augusta, Georgia, a count from 1852 showed a total population of 10,217, with a White population of 5,256 (about 51%), and an African American population of 4,961, of whom only 243 (about 5% of the Black population) were free.[33]

Education for African American children had been available, very sparingly, in Washington, D. C. since the second decade of the 1800s, but in light of the statistics, the opportunity for George Monroe to attend school was exceedingly rare. The census of 1850 for the state of Maryland counted 26,590 Black children, about

1,600 (6.1%) of whom attended school. Ten years later, the 1860 census for Maryland would count 30,110 Black children with school enrollment dropping to 4.5%.[34]

George and his uncle would remain in Washington, D.C. for as long as two years, waiting for news from California. Meanwhile, thirty-two-year-old Mary, traveling alone, bravely undertook the three-week-long journey from New York to California. Arriving in San Francisco, then taking a riverboat into central California, she would likely have rolled into Calaveras County by horse-drawn stage a few days later.

If Mary had passed through San Francisco by the first of 1854, she may have glimpsed the newly-promoted Captain Ulysses S. Grant as he boarded a steamer en route to Fort Humboldt, 250 miles to the north. Grant and Louis Monroe, now both living in Northern California and separated from their families, appear to have dealt with their circumstances in similarly self-destructive ways: Grant with alcohol, and Monroe with "recklessness," and both would eventually overcome these predilections through the encouragement of their wives.[35]

Travel-weary and patinaed with road dust, as soon as Mary stepped off the stage and received her baggage, her next move would have been to find Louis. One can barely imagine her consternation, after weeks of dangerous and difficult travel, as she inquired around her unsavory and often alarming surroundings only to find that her husband wasn't anywhere to be seen. But consternation would have given way to something far more vivid when she finally learned what had become of him.

Louis had heard that his wife was coming to see him, but rather than greeting her at the stage platform, he appears to have fled in a panic. His brother-in-law George Millen told the story:

"Her husband was so excited, when he heard she was here, he got up and left the county he was in. She followed him, and when she got to him and everything became reconciled, she took hold and managed everything, and made her peace. They lived together in Mariposa. I remained in Washington, D. C. and kept her son at school, and then I came and brought him here."[36]

The iron-willed Mary had somehow tracked her husband eighty miles south, probably by stage from Calaveras County to Mariposa, which would have taken at least two days' travel. Whether she cornered him in one of the several saloons in town, or while he was cutting somebody's hair, the encounter must have been rather dramatic. Whatever was said, Mary persuaded Louis to accept his responsibilities as a husband and father and let his wife handle their affairs.

Across the country in Washington, D.C., it was once again time for George Monroe and his uncle to pack their belongings for another long trip. It is estimated that some four thousand African Americans headed for California during the Gold Rush, and nine-year-old George was joining them. Accompanied by his uncle and a shipload of adventurous travelers, this would be the experience of a lifetime, following the route his father and mother had taken and reuniting with them in Mariposa.[37]

Travelers bound for California generally boarded their steamships in New York harbor. Though steamers sometimes made stops down the east coast in Charleston and Savannah for mail and coal, they were likely to already have full loads with no room to pick up additional passengers. It is unlikely that George's uncle and parents would have chosen the months-long trip around Cape Horn to San Francisco. Given the general timeline laid out in Millen's later testimony, they probably used the shorter route through Nicaragua (4,700 miles), or via the Isthmus of Panama (5,224 miles). Ulysses S. Grant had taken the latter route in 1852. By 1855 those routes generally took twenty-two to twenty-four days, at a cost per person of around $110, or roughly $3,800 in current dollars as estimated by online calculators, and about half the price of a ticket for the dangerous and grueling overland stagecoach trip.[38]

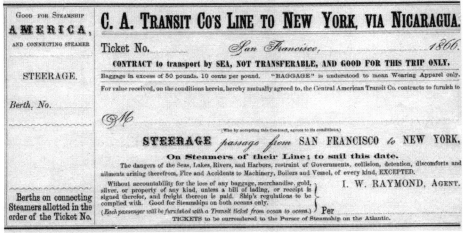

1866 Ticket, San Francisco to New York via Nicaragua
(Author's Collection)[39]

For Grant, the steamship passage from New York to Aspinwall (now Colón, Panama) took eight days. According to Grant:

"At that time the streets of the town were eight or ten inches under water, and foot passengers passed from place to place on raised foot-walks. July is at the height of the wet season, on the Isthmus. At intervals the rain would pour down in streams, followed in not many minutes by a blazing, tropical summers sun. These alternate changes, from rain to sunshine, were continuous in the afternoons. I wondered how any person could live many months in Aspinwall, and wondered still more why any one tried.

In the summer of 1852 the Panama railroad was completed only to the point where it now crosses the Chagres River. From there passengers were carried by boats to Gorgona, at which place they took mules for Panama [City], some twenty-five miles further."[40]

If taking the Nicaragua route, the two Georges would have landed at Greytown, Nicaragua, transferred to a steamer on the San Juan River to and across Lake Nicaragua, then overland a dozen miles to the Pacific Ocean. Or, choosing the Panama route, they may have taken the new railroad (finished in 1855) to shorten the trip.[41]

George and his uncle are reported to have arrived in Mariposa one year after Mary, whose fateful reunion with Louis is variously recorded as 1854 or 1855. That would suggest that the year of George Monroe's journey to California was either 1855 or '56. Still in his first decade of life, George Monroe had racked up some considerable experiences, leaving his extended family in Georgia, living in the nation's capital and attending school, seeing New York City, sailing to Central America and San Francisco, then traveling overland into Gold Rush California. His story thus far, while remarkable, is very much in step with that of his extraordinary family.[42]

George Millen, after seeing his sister, nephew, and brother-in-law settled in Mariposa, would head back up the state, wandering far north of Calaveras County and finally settling in the Trinity County town of Weaverville, California, where he would spend the next twenty years before returning to Mariposa.[43]

Chapter II

MARIPOSA—*The Monroes settle in Mariposa, California. Yosemite draws increasing tourism.*

Louis and Mary chose a home in town, probably within walking distance of Main Street, where Louis would set up shop as a barber. George Millen may have stuck around to help ease the family's transition to their new surroundings, perhaps getting work as a blacksmith, and continuing to mentor his nephew while Louis and Mary worked to establish their home and income. But Millen, the self-professed rover, would soon head up to the northern California mines and leave his capable sister to, as he later characterized it, "manage everything."[44]

Young George Monroe was once again having to deal with a stark transition in his way of living. Though reunited with his mother and father, George may have experienced a bit of culture-shock after trading Washington, D.C. for Mariposa. There would be no more school for him; public schools only enrolled White children. On occasion, an informal private school might be established in a local residence, but whether the Monroes were able to find a teacher for George remains undiscovered.

Though Mariposa may have been an arbitrary destination for Louis when he fled his wife's arrival in Calaveras County, the newish town had enough anti-slavery Republicans in it to offer some attraction for an African American family. The local newspaper leaned Republican, as did a fair portion of the resident miners, and there was a sprinkling of Black families around the area. This could have given the Monroes new hope for their future, in contrast to the bleak outlook they had faced during their time in Georgia, surrounded by the culture of slavery.

The only written description of George's critical formative years, from age ten to nineteen, appears in his obituary: "As he grew to manhood he tired of the monotony of town life." But he did find other attractions more suited to his personality. The same article indicates that George emerged from his teen years having developed "a natural taste for horsebreaking, riding and driving team ...." In his pre-teens, whether helping his mother at home or his father at work, George would have had plenty to do. The Monroe home might likely have had a vegetable garden, chickens for eggs, and a dairy cow. During these years George's affinity toward animals would certainly have shown through.[45]

The reference to George's "natural taste for horsebreaking" may be misleading to the reader. Many successful equestrians object to the concept of horse-breaking, as one famous trainer put it, "The connotation is to break the horse's spirit in order to dominate the horse and bend its will to the trainer's by a struggle." Instead, Monroe appears to have learned, or intuited, the gentler approach favored by latter-day trainers. A later reminiscence speaks to his personal connection with horses, describing Monroe as knowing his horses' names, speaking to them in mostly pleasant tones, and refraining from the use of a whip. As a boy, George likely took care of the family horse and perhaps got work as a stable-hand in one of the many nearby livery stables.[46]

Taking along the family dog, George would have shared adventures with his father, learning to hunt, fish, and navigate the hills and streams of the Sierra foothills. Educated by his parents as time allowed, reading material was available in the form of the newspaper and the family Bible, and assignments could include writing letters to his Uncle George and Grandmother Polly. As his immediate role-models, George's parents were active, social, and keenly focused on securing their place in the community. Sharing the local news may very well have been a primary source of interest for the whole family, if not the entire town. As it turns out, there was a good deal of history being made, locally and nationally, all of which would deeply influence the life of George Monroe.

1856 was just one year after several tourist parties of non-Indigenous travelers first ventured into Yosemite Valley from Mariposa on horseback. The profundity of their impressions of what they had seen in Yosemite, reported internationally through various publications, alerted the world that California's gold was not the only attraction to the state. Yosemite brought widespread attention to the Monroes' little mining town. Mariposa had become a portal for nothing less than a spiritual pilgrimage for world-travelers, and in ten years George Monroe would become their guide.

It would take all of ten years, not only for George to grow to manhood, but also for the very nature of his future career to materialize. Paving the way toward that future, there were plenty of work-hardened entrepreneurs on hand who saw the possibilities of the new scenic attraction, and through their efforts would invent the local industry that would furnish employment for George and many others. Yet to be built were the trails, waystations, and transportation systems that would enable mass-visitation to Yosemite. But for the present, the Monroes' efforts had all to do with Louis getting work in town, and together establishing a suitable home for the family. At nine years old, George Monroe was on the cusp of another wildly improbable future that would gradually unfold before his eyes, and welcome him at the very moment he was ready to embrace it.

Some local residents, either unaware or uninterested in the fact that earlier inhabitants had already named the place "Ahwahnee," bickered about the pronunciation of their newly appropriated name of Yosemite, as reported in the local paper:

CLARK'S PIONEER CABIN AT WAWONA
[From a sketch made for the CHRONICLE by Thomas Hill.]

Clark's Station, c. 1866, showing an extension to the left of an improved
version of the earlier cabin (Author Collection)[47]

"How shall the great valley, by some called the Yo Semite and by others Yo Hamite, be spelled and pronounced. Will some learned savant or rabbi, acquainted with the [Indigenous] idiom and pronunciation, please indicate and oblige."[48]

One of the locals, Galen Clark, had just taken out a pre-emption claim on 160 acres at what was being called Clark's Crossing. Located midway on the route from Mariposa to Yosemite, the "crossing" was a relatively wide and shallow section along the South Fork of the Merced River. Here Clark would establish a hotel business that would evolve under a succession of names, including Clark's Ferry, Clark's Ranch, Clark's Station, Clark & Moore's, Big Tree Station, and, finally, the Wawona Hotel.

Clark's humble beginning was described by James H. Lawrence in the *San Francisco Chronicle*, June 1895:

"In April, 1857, Clark … built his first cabin near the crossing. It was constructed on the old frontier American plan, with the chimney outside and a roof of 'shakes,' held in place by 'weight-poles,' the logs unhewn and substantial in size. The structure was sixteen by twelve feet outside, and its location was nearly in front of the dining-room of the present [Wawona] hotel, or between that point and the studio of Thomas Hill, the artist, who recently sketched the old cabin from a description given by Clark."[49]

In 1857, not far from his new home, Clark found a grove of giant sequoia trees (now called the Mariposa Grove of Giant Sequoias) and eagerly shared the news of its existence. The local paper immediately launched a rivalry with the Calaveras Grove to the north:

"We have often heard of this collection of shrubs known as the mammoth grove of Calaveras … that patch of undergrowth … dwarfish bushes …. We regret that we are unable to give … a correct estimate of the height of the tallest of our trees, owing to the fact that during our visit the intervening clouds prevented our seeing anything above the lower limbs."[50]

Probably the first reported anecdote from the Monroe family shows up the next year, in December 1858, as readers of the *Mariposa Gazette* were treated to a drama featuring George's dad and the family dog:

"Mr. L. A. Monroe was hunting quail on Wednesday, within one mile of this place, when his dog, a fine Pointer, came suddenly upon a large buck, who seemed to consider himself proprietor of that immediate vicinity, and, so charged upon the dog. —He struck him with his horns; one of which, penetrated into the fore shoulder of the dog six inches, and then broke off leaving that portion of the horn in the wound. Monroe coming up near, the buck then left."[51]

The fate of the dog remains unreported. The very fact that this incident made it into the *Gazette* is an early indication that the publisher, Lemuel Albert Holmes, was acquainted with Monroe — Louis may have shared his story while giving Holmes a haircut. Beyond that, the article is reported in a respectful manner, in contrast to the newspaper's occasional anecdotes depicting African Americans as objects of comic derision. Monroe's connection with the *Mariposa Gazette* would continue and deepen over the years to come.[52]

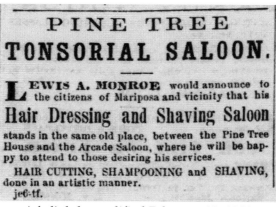

PINE TREE

TONSORIAL SALOON.

LEWIS A. MONROE

BEING one of the unfortunates by the late fire, has re-opened a new and completely arranged

Hair Dressing and Shaving Saloon,

And announces to the public that his facilities for performing all work pertaining to the profession, are unsurpassed.

HAIR CUTTING, SHAMPOONING and SHAVING, done in an artistic manner.

☞ Saloon in McNamarra's Building.

je6-tf.

January 1, 1861

An advertisement indicates that by 1858 Louis had a barbershop in Mariposa. In January 1861, while page two of the *Gazette* covers events that would lead to civil war, the front page reveals Louis Monroe's livelihood. His new business would be called the Pine Tree Tonsorial Saloon, located at 5th Street and Main (now state highway 49), in the McNamara Building that also housed a small hotel called the Pine Tree House, and the Arcade Saloon. The "late fire" mentioned in his advertisement probably refers back to the conflagration of June 1858, which destroyed Mariposa's entire business district and evidently impacted Monroe. [53]

PINE TREE

TONSORIAL SALOON.

LEWIS A. MONROE would announce to the citizens of Mariposa and vicinity that his

Hair Dressing and Shaving Saloon

stands in the same old place, between the Pine Tree House and the Arcade Saloon, where he will be happy to attend to those desiring his services.

HAIR CUTTING, SHAMPOONING and SHAVING, done in an artistic manner.

je6-tf.

Ad slightly modified February 12, 1861

As a barber in the center of Mariposa, Monroe was in a great position to socialize, hear the latest gossip, and make friends. Monroe's principal clientele may have been miners—census data from nine years earlier show 71% of Mariposa's population listing themselves as such. But the census also showed plenty of others who were part of the local economy. In 1850 there were listed 6 bank owners, 4 blacksmiths, 18 carpenters, 6 men who gave their profession as "Catching Wild Horses," 10 cooks, 15 farmers, 40 merchants, and a man named Blas Castro who gave his profession as "Gambler." In all, 77 were entered as "M" for Mulatto (as were the Monroes later on), and 20 as "B" for Black.[54]

At the end of July 1861, the *Gazette* announced an event revealing a bit of the town's character:

> "A complimentary Ball will take place this evening at Concert Hall, for the benefit of Mr. Wm. Crocker. Mr. C. has been residing for many years in this county; the greater portion of his time, however, has been spent in this town, where crowds would nightly congregate at his saloon to hear his able executions on the piano. We hope our citizens, in order to show their gratitude for his many kindnesses will turn out and give him a full house."[55]

Though musical events such as Crocker's may have brought the citizens of Mariposa together, there remained an underlying tension among them, reflecting the polarization of the entire country. On Tuesday morning, December 17, 1861, readers of the *Gazette*, including the Monroes, could contemplate a nearly full-page update from President Lincoln regarding the "peculiar exigencies of the times" caused by a "disloyal portion of the American people [who] have, during the whole year, been engaged in an attempt to divide and destroy the Union."

On page two, following Lincoln's statements, the *Gazette* offered two side-by-side columns expressing the conflicting attitudes about slavery underlying the Civil War. On one hand, the first declared, "The danger threatening the institution of Slavery, from the temporary success of the Republican party, formed the excuse for 'firing the Southern heart' ...." On the other hand, the second stated, "The Free School system, a blessing when properly conducted, has been made the medium of inculcating into the tender mind impracticable theories in reference to Slavery and a religious hatred of slaveholders."[56]

Reading such articles lamenting the disparagement of slaveholders, Mary Monroe would have felt concern for her mother and extended family who were still in the south, but relief for having removed her immediate family to the west. Still, political and social polarization surrounded the Monroes. While giving shaves, haircuts, and shampoos in his tonsorial saloon, Louis must have endured ample servings of strong opinion from all sides. In order to keep his customers, Louis would have had to employ considerable diplomacy, measuring and refining his thoughts and comments. Indeed, the barbershop was an ideal classroom for Louis, who was gaining skills that would later serve him as an advocate for Black civil rights.

Major General Ulysses S. Grant was likewise refining his thoughts along lines that would directly mesh with those of Louis Monroe—thoughts that would probably have fallen under the *Gazette* contributor's category of "impracticable theories in reference to slavery." In November of 1862 amidst the raging conflict, Grant evidenced his extraordinary prescience, outlining to his colleague, John Eaton, a vision for the systematic enfranchisement of the thousands escaping enslavement as northern armies advanced. After outlining how to employ formerly enslaved men and women as a paid labor force for the Union, Grant " ... then went on to say that when it had been made clear that the negro as an independent laborer could do these things well, it would be very easy to put a musket in his hands and make a soldier of him, and if he fought well, eventually to put the ballot in his hand and make him a citizen." Though dismissed by some as impracticable, essential elements of Grant's vision would in the coming years be effectively implemented by Louis, Mary, and George Monroe.[57]

As a teenager, George ranged through the local foothills, fishing, hunting, exploring, and evidently keeping a sharp eye out for the very specific element that had brought his family to California—gold. 1862 started off with ten feet of snow blanketing the mountains just east of Mariposa, promising a brisk spring runoff. George may have known to monitor the local ephemeral streams as they began to swell in late winter, washing away silt and rocks and occasionally revealing an overlooked treasure. That March found George on a ramble south of Mariposa, about four-hundred yards north-east of Mariposa Creek. He was, maybe not by chance, in the vicinity of perhaps the oldest stamp mill in California, erected in 1849 to pulverize gold-bearing quartz. While George may have been hunting or fishing for that evening's family dinner, something must have caught his eye, prompting him to reach into an icy rushing creek to pull out a bit of rock. Heading home, instead of merely bringing in fish or quail, George handed the family a windfall, meriting a blurb in the papers:

"Last week George Monroe picked up in Quartz gulch near town, a piece of quartz and gold which yielded on pounding up, $273, as is stated."[58]

Online calculators estimate George's find in current dollars (2023) to be over $8,000.[59]

Spring of 1863 brought new optimism for the Union; Grant, after repeated successes in battle, was formally promoted by

Lincoln to the exalted rank of Lieutenant General. The Monroes had further cause for optimism: seven years after their tenuous arrival in Mariposa, they were now well-known, established residents, and it appears that part of Mary's program to rehabilitate her family had included some effective financial planning. With the funds she had brought from Georgia, and the success of Louis' Tonsorial Saloon (and George's newfound gold), the Monroes conceived a plan to establish their own ranch, or farm, outside of town.

In September 1863, Louis applied for a homestead claim about six miles to the southeast. It was good farmland, but after filing the claim they made no move to develop or live on the property, so the claim eventually expired. With the Civil War still raging, the Monroes' aspirations to land ownership may have been premature. The federal government had not yet recognized African Americans as equal citizens, and even though the Homestead Act of 1862 had no racial restrictions, the Monroes' homestead claim may have struck officials as too radically progressive.[60]

Change was coming, though, and whatever the reason for their inaction, seven years later the Monroes will have homesteaded and developed a 160-acre farm-ranch adjacent to the claim they'd previously abandoned. During those seven years, Ulysses S. Grant would carry the Union Army to victory in the American Civil War, ascend to the presidency, and pave the way for many of the Monroe family's future achievements through his energetic backing of constitutional rights for African Americans.[61]

EMANCIPATION—*Slavery in post-war California. Reconstruction brings new opportunities to the Monroes. Louis Monroe becomes a pillar of the local Black community, and George shows an affinity for horses.*

In 1865, Congress passed the Thirteenth Amendment to the United States Constitution, abolishing slavery. It would be ratified by the State of California that December. By this time, it was apparent that Louis Monroe had long since abandoned his "reckless" past, and was a respectable, involved citizen. Monroe had subscribed to *The Elevator*, a San Francisco newspaper established in 1865 to report on issues of interest to African Americans throughout the west coast. In July, Monroe had signed up as the Mariposa agent for the paper, effectively making himself a hub of communication between the local African American community and the outside world. He would continue his association with the newspaper for at least the next ten years.

As George Monroe approached his eighteenth year, he would have been in the process of defining himself as a young adult. He was certainly developing into a competent horseman. Later descriptions show he enjoyed racing and might have been a bit of a daredevil in a carriage, reportedly flying around corners with the carriage-wheels on one side completely airborne. George could race through the foothills, confident and free, in unity with his equine friends feeling the wind in their faces and the galloping power of youth.

He had two strong role models to help him along—his stalwart mother and his increasingly interesting father. George was privy to his father's stories from work, which provided a deep well of vicarious experience from which to learn. In those days before the many passive diversions of the twentieth century, George and his parents could have had the time to discuss local news, comparing it with reports from *The Elevator*. During his parents' attempt to acquire farmland, the teenager would have ruminated over his future role and how he, personally, fit into the overall picture. Would he be a farmer, or would he learn a trade as his uncle and father had? Would the optimistic news out of Washington, D.C. signal the emergence of new possibilities?

In August of 1865, *The Elevator* received a letter from Louis Monroe indicating his and others' interest in having Mariposa County represented at the upcoming "Colored Convention" in Sacramento.[62]

Monroe then took action. In September the *Gazette* reported:

> "The colored people had a mass meeting in this place on last Tuesday evening [September 12]. Quite a large number were present. L. A. Monroe was chosen Chairman, with a Secretary whose name we did not ascertain. Moses Rogers was chosen delegate from this county to the State Convention. A series of resolutions was passed—some remarks were made by various of those present, and the Convention, after a very orderly session, adjourned."[63]

Their "very orderly session" likely belied some strong emotion among the attendees. During the Civil War, California had a robust secession movement in support of slavery. Slavery had been banned in California by its constitution in 1849; nonetheless, it is estimated that by 1865 there may have been as many as a thousand people of African descent enslaved in California.[64]

Mariposa's delegate for the upcoming convention, Moses Rodgers (aka "Rogers") had firsthand knowledge of the situation in the nearby mining district of Hornitos, just a few miles from Mariposa. Born into enslavement in Missouri, Rodgers had managed to achieve a prestigious reputation as a mining engineer in Hornitos by the 1860s. One account suggests that Rodgers may have come to California in 1849 from Texas as one of several enslaved by Colonel Thomas Thorn.

Moses Rodgers (Mariposa Museum and History Center Collection)

Accounts of Thorn's experiences leading up to and including his time in the Mariposa area present a vivid picture of the social climate surrounding the Monroe family. Originally from New Jersey, Thorn had been a successful cotton planter in Little Rock, Arkansas before moving in 1844 to the farming and ranching settlement of Keechi Creek, Texas, where forced labor was carried out by enslaved people.[65]

In 1850, the county surrounding Keechi Creek counted 621 enslaved African Americans; by 1855, the number would swell to 1,455 with an estimated value on the slavery market of $757,296 (in 1855 dollars), far exceeding the taxable value of the land. In 1849, lured by gold, Thorn sold his land and, taking a "large number of slaves" together with his family and friends joined a train of 200 wagons along the southern route to California via New Mexico and Arizona.[66]

The Thorn party spent the winter of 1849-50 in Los Angeles. During that time, according to a Los Angeles police report, two men enslaved by Thorn attempted to "assert their rights to freedom," evidently aware that California's new constitution outlawed slavery. They appear to have escaped, but not before one, Allen Sanford, was made victim to an "assault and battery," and the other, Stephen Cribbs, was "shot at," in both cases by Thorn or his traveling companions.[67]

A Los Angeles police officer named J. H. Purdy filed a complaint against Thorn on behalf of Cribbs and Sanford, but according to the report:

"[Officer Purdy] was ordered by a committee of five, appointed by a meeting of Americans, to leave town within twenty-four hours. He appealed to the authorities for protection, but they were unable to give it, and was forced to leave at the designated time. Mob law, to use the harsh but truthful term, is triumphant as regards the existence of negro slavery in this district."[68]

Thorn settled that spring in Hornitos with his family and the remainder of those he'd enslaved, but with the apparent absence of Stephen Cribbs and Allen Sanford. The Thorn Household entry in the 1850 census lists ten "Servants," five "Black" (three of whom have "Thorn" as their last name), and five "Mulatto." Listed as "White" are Thorn and his wife and three children, along with a miner, a merchant, and a physician.

Moses Rodgers, then 13 years old, is not named in the household group, but not all those enslaved by Thorn were included on the list. Early in 1850, there was an incident involving Thorn that Rodgers may have been involved in, or at least could have known about. According to the same report that had documented the escape of Cribbs and Sanford in Los Angeles: "The remainder of the slaves were taken up to the mines finally, but the white miners stampeded them; they all ran away, and their owners did not get even the cost of bringing them here." Thus, in the space of a few months, Thorn had received two starkly contrasting verdicts regarding his slaveholding, both delivered by "mob law" and demonstrating the violent polarization that existed in California and the entire country.

Despite intimidation by local anti-slavery miners, Thorn, ignoring state law, continued to enslave people, including one Peter Green (also not mentioned in the 1850 census). Pro-slavery lawmakers called "Chivalry Democrats," had succeeded in passing legislation to undermine California's constitutional restriction on slavery. Through their efforts, the California Fugitive Slave Act of 1852 allowed Thorn to enslave people under legal contracts. According to one such contract from February 1853: "I Thomas Thorn ... being the rightful owner of the Negro man Peter Green and entitled to his service as a slave during his life ...." agreed to release Green provided that he "shall pay to me the sum of one thousand dollars, good lawful money or work for and serve me from present time until one year from and after the first day of April next being until the first day of April A.D. 1854."[69]

Green wasn't released on the agreed-upon date, or even upon Thorn's death in November 1854, indicating that Green had been inherited by Thorn's wife, Mary, and was still enslaved by the family. While Green may have been pressed into labor in the mines, others worked for Mary in running the Thorn home as a boardinghouse for miners and travelers. One local miner named Charles Davis wrote that at one time when Mary was ill, there was "nobody except the Old [Black] Woman & her two daughters to serve up for the boarders."[70]

There is evidence that residents had separated themselves both ideologically and geographically from their neighbors in Mariposa, settling eighteen miles to the west in Hornitos, in a community of like-minded neighbors. In 1856 an upstart newspaper called the *Mariposa Democrat* went into competition with the Republican-leaning *Gazette*. A year after its debut in Mariposa, the *Democrat* moved its offices to Hornitos, complaining of local political favoritism:

> "The whole of the county printing has been given over to the Gazette since the issuing of the Democrat, and as this is the principal source of revenue to a party paper, why, nothing beneficial could result to us from longer remaining in Mariposa Town."[71]

Thus removed from their Republican rivals, the *Democrat* railed against the "profligacy and corruption" of abolitionist Republicans and printed a slur-filled anecdote about a local Black miner who supposedly rebuked two abolitionists by telling them how well-treated he was.[72]

Peter Green's release from forced servitude was finally signed by Mariposa Justice of the Peace James Givens in August 1855:

> "In the presence of Benjamine F. Ropp, P. Cadell, jr., Joseph A Tiry I hereby notify that the above obligation has been

49

complied with and that Peter Green was legally discharged."[73]

Moses Rodgers, through his association with Louis Monroe, had entered the circle of strong, inspirational role models for young George Monroe, showing by example how an African American man might negotiate the twisted pathways of the local environment. By 1864, Rodgers had become one of the most successful mining engineers in Hornitos. He and a business partner were running the nearby Washington Mine, once reported to have produced 1,000 ounces of gold per day. Thomas Thorn's sons had remained in the area and continued to work the mines, side by side with formerly enslaved people and workers from a multitude of other countries, including China and Mexico.

According to writer Newell D. Chamberlain, " … freed slaves generally stayed in close proximity to their former masters and so, after the Civil War, there were fifteen or twenty Negro families, living near the southern limits of Hornitos." A photograph of Hornitos "old-timers" from 1890 shows Moses Rodgers posing together with Thorn's son.[74]

By 1865 Louis Monroe had made the acquaintance of Moses Rodgers, perhaps at the barbershop, or through Monroe's role as an agent for *The Elevator*. Positioned at the hub of the Black community and main-street Mariposa, Louis was well-situated to grasp the complexity and nuance of the current social and political climate. At home, the teenaged George Monroe might have been included in his parents' discussion of local issues. There was plenty to talk about: Moses Rodgers' interactions with former slaveholders, the unfamiliar customs of various local ethnic communities, cautionary tales about discriminatory treatment, people and places to avoid, President Lincoln's assassination, and ongoing news coming out of Washington, D.C., where George had attended school ten years before. With the war's end and the

Reconstruction Era at hand, African Americans would experience unprecedented freedom and rights, and here in the little mining town of Mariposa, George Monroe would have a front-row seat from which to experience the coming changes.[75]

Re-union of old-timers at Hornitos in front of Ralph Wood Barcroft's Hornitos Saloon, 1890. Left to right, front row: R. Barcroft, Al Sylvester, Sam Collier, Joe Spagnoli, Nat Bailey, Tom Thorn [son of Col. Thomas Thorn], Robert Arthur, and Tom Williams. Rear row: Henry Nelson, Smith Thomas, John Branson, William Dennis, B. A. Shepard, G. Gagliardo, J. D. Craighan, M. L. Rodgers.[76]

One month after the September "mass meeting" in Mariposa under Louis Monroe's chairmanship, Moses Rodgers traveled to Sacramento to represent his county at the California State Convention of Colored Citizens, serving on the "Committee on Industrial Pursuits." Included in the many Resolutions adopted by Rodgers' committee:

" … we recommend the colored people of the Pacific States and Territories to secure farms, purchase homesteads, enter largely into quartz and other branches of mining, engage in mechanical and manufacturing occupations and eagerly embrace every method and opportunity which will insure profit, honor and independence.

… we urge upon the people of this coast to seek unsettled lands and pre-empt them, as is the right of every American citizen … we hail with joy inexpressible, as one of the practical movements of the freedmen, their settled and persistent determination to become owners of the soil …."[77]

The Monroes' aborted attempt to pre-empt farmland in 1863 may have inspired Rodgers to include the latter recommendation, which in turn may have prompted Louis and Mary to reconsider the matter. Far more inspiration was to be found in the fascinating document published by *The Elevator*, *Proceedings of the California State Convention of Colored Citizens, Held in Sacramento on the 25th, 26th, 27th, and 28th of October, 1865*. It provides a glimpse into the African American perspective on race relations and civil rights in California at the time, alternately optimistic, practical, and radical:

[Page 3]: "Rev. O. M. Briggs, Agent for the Freedmen's Bureau for the Pacific coast stated: … We must expect opposition, even from Union men; the country was fast coming up to that point when equal political rights would be awarded to colored men, not only as a reward for their valor, patriotism and loyalty, but as justly due them as men and citizens. He likewise said that prejudice was fast abating on this coast.

[Page 6] The law should be amended so as to give to every child the privileges of education. If there were not to have a separate school, let them be admitted to those already established. As a law-abiding and tax-paying class we are entitled to greater advantages in this respect than we now enjoy, and which it is unfair to deprive us of.

[Page 8]: *Resolved*—That we rejoice that this war has resulted in the overthrow of slavery, and its total extinction by Federal legislation, in an amendment to the Constitution.

Resolved—That we have a new love for the American Union, and shall ever willingly lay down our lives in defense of the great principles of our Republic ....

[Page 9]: *Resolved*—That no Christian nation with any real sense of justice or humanity, could ask a class of people to assist in saving the Government from destruction, and after they had sacrificed hundreds and thousands of their lives to that effect, to then deny them of the common rights that nature has endowed them with; rights involving principles upon which the Government founded its political institutions, pronounced by them to be the natural rights of all men ....

[Page 11]: Mr. Moore urged that the time had arrived for men to speak out boldly, and let the world know what we think as men. He is opposed to anything like cringing. We have a perfect right to read and criticize the acts of our Government.

[Page 11]: Resolved—That we sympathize with the Fenian movement to liberate Ireland from the yoke of British bondage, and when we have obtained our full citizenship in this country, we should be willing to assist our Irish brethren in their struggle for National Independence; and 40,000 colored troops could be raised to butt the horns off the hypocritical English bull." [This resolution was not passed].[78]

An amendment to the state Constitution to allow Black men the right to vote was also proposed by the convention. The published *Proceedings*, filled with promise and purpose, must have made exciting and heady reading for the Monroes. Still, George, close to his 18th birthday, may have shaken his head with irony at the news that Black children might be admitted to public schools, now too late for his own benefit.

The post-war era found the Monroes in a stimulating, though somewhat bewildering, social milieu with a rainbow of ethnicities and the peculiar juxtaposition of families living and working alongside those they had formerly enslaved. Within this environment, Louis and Mary Monroe were able to make deliberate and successful application of each new freedom that emerged during post-war Reconstruction. Their efforts would carry the family forward and sustain them for years to come.

In November 1865, a follow-up meeting in Mariposa was reported in *The Elevator*:

"A public meeting of the colored citizens of Mariposa was held on Tuesday evening, November 21st ... to hear the report of Mr. Moses L. Rogers, the delegate to the Convention from Mariposa.

Mr. Rogers on being called upon responded in an eloquent address, in which he urged union and action by the colored people of this county, and throughout the entire State, in order to secure our rights and to carry out the work the Convention has commenced. We had begun battling for our

rights as citizens, and we must not give up the work, but continue until it is completed. We must use every available means to develop our abilities, and convince the Anglo Saxon race that we are capable of exercising our political rights, and are fully entitled to 'Equality before the law.'
Moved, by L. A. Monroe, that in accordance with the recommendation of the Convention, we elect a County Executive Committee, auxiliary to the State Executive Committee. Carried ...."

Among the several reported resolutions at the meeting:

"Moved, by E. Quivers, that we celebrate the Third Anniversary of President Lincoln's Emancipation Proclamation, on the first of January next .... Moved, by M. L. Rogers, that the celebration conclude with a grand ball."[79]

Both motions were carried.

Chapter III

SETTING THE STAGE—*Galen Clark, Henry Washburn, and the travel industry.*

If one could visit with George Monroe around this time, perhaps fishing along a peaceful section of Mariposa Creek, and ask him how he envisioned his future, he might very reasonably point out that his life so far had been so unpredictable that he couldn't rightly say. As it turns out, his future would continue to flow, like Mariposa Creek, down unforeseeable paths. The stars were slowly beginning to align for George, and though the trajectories of events were set, they would have been too gradual and apparently disconnected for George to have perceived their import.

Though the idea of post-war reconstruction offered a glimmer of hope, employment opportunities for African Americans remained quite narrow. At the 1865 convention, Moses Rodgers gave employment statistics for the 62 Black residents he'd counted in Mariposa County:

"Number of Families–10
 Children–20
 Quartz Miners–10
 Placer Miners–20
 Ranchers–5
 Blacksmiths–2
 Barbers–2
 Painter–1
 Boot-maker–1
 Tailor–1
 Estimated value of property-$20,000"[80]

In an environment of overt, systemic discrimination, every woman and non-White male could expect to be barred from all but a very few avenues for advancement. Andrew Johnson, having taken his place as president after Lincoln's assassination, declared, "This is a country for white men, and, by God, while I am president it shall be a government for white men."[81]

The idea that George could achieve the envied status of stage-driver would have barely merited consideration; it seems more likely that George would set his sights on his uncle's profession as a blacksmith.

Thus far, the circle of influence upon George's life had been confined mostly to his immediate family, but a couple of people whom he would have noticed around town soon joined that circle, including one sturdy, bearded man called Galen Clark. Clark had journeyed into Yosemite Valley ten years before and was now running his tiny hotel halfway between that place and Mariposa. Clark had introduced a slowly increasing trickle of guests to the nearby giant sequoias and Yosemite. Over time, some of those guests had joined with Clark in conceiving a plan to guard the trees and valley from damage. Through their efforts, in 1864 Yosemite Valley and the Mariposa Grove of Big Trees came under protection by a piece of federal legislation called the Yosemite Grant, signed into law by Abraham Lincoln. The text of the legislation specified that the land would be preserved for "public use, resort, and recreation."

Galen Clark, his hotel, and his support for the innovation that created Yosemite Park would all be essential elements in the next phase of George Monroe's life. In addition to Clark, there was another, younger man about town named Washburn who may have appeared to George as just one of many entrepreneurs trying to get a leg up in the mining business. But that man was getting ready to change jobs, just as the town was about to change its economic base, largely because of Galen Clark. And as a result, George was about to find his career.

To fully set the stage for George's future would take a couple more years, during which a new industry would spring up and hand George the opportunity of a lifetime. Here's how it unfolded.

In April 1866, a catastrophic fire once again destroyed the business district of Mariposa, including Louis Monroe's Pine Tree Tonsorial Saloon. Having survived the Mariposa fire of 1858, Monroe once again maintained his livelihood through the disaster and would see his business resume in a new building at the same location on the north-east corner of 5th Street and Main.[82]

Schlageter Hotel (Author photograph)

In December of that year, the *Gazette* announced:

"The New Hotel.
… We have seen the design of the building, sketched by the hand of the ingenious Snediker …. [It] will have frontage on

Main street of fifty two feet with an extreme depth into Fifth street, of eighty six feet. The house will be of brick and fire proof, and will contain in all twenty rooms, including one large dining saloon, thirty four feet by twenty one. ... It will have a commodious bar room, well provided with a stock of prime lager and sundry other drinkables we presume, a sitting room for gentlemen and a parlor for ladies, with separate entrances from Main street.

At one end Professor Monroe will have his 'studio' and will there ply the instruments of the 'tonsorial art,' on the facial anatomy of his patrons or relieve them of any incumbrance in the shape of hair. It is almost needless to say that the proprietor and High Priest of this embryo establishment is the indefatigable [Herman] Schlageter .... The building is rising rapidly into shape and with anything like favorable weather we may look to for completion by the end of January next."[83]

During the same month, a presidential veto from Andrew Johnson was overridden by Congress, resulting in the enactment of the Civil Rights Act of 1866, giving citizenship to Black Americans and guaranteeing equal rights with Whites. Congress also created six Army regiments of African Americans, now known as the Buffalo Soldiers, some of whom would later serve to protect Yosemite National Park in 1899, 1903, and 1904.[84]

Mariposa 1870. The Mariposa County Courthouse (with its prominent bell-tower) is visible top-left-of-center, and the cube-shaped two-story building fronting the street (in a direct line below the courthouse) is the Schlageter Hotel. An uncorroborated caption accompanying the picture in an early 20th century Washburn family album reads: "The four men lived in the cabin at left side of picture. They are L to R: Henry Washburn, Chas. or Herman Schlageter, John Washburn & Jim Barrett." (Author collection and Yosemite Museum and Archives)[85]

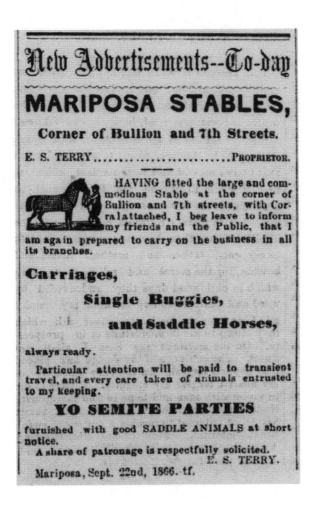

Also reported among the losses from the Mariposa fire were the
stable & home of Colonel E. S. Terry, estimated at $9,000. Terry had
run a livery stable in town since 1860, offering guided tourist
excursions to Yosemite by saddle-train. After the fire he rebuilt his
business, moving a block up from Main Street between 6th and 7th
to Bullion and 7th.[86]

But only a year later, Terry's business would have a new owner:

"A Transfer.—We understand that A. H. Washburn has concluded arrangements with Col. Terry to buy out the latter's extensive livery stable. Mr. Washburn will now carry on the business in all its branches, and will do his best to merit equal patronage to that extended to his predecessor. We wish him every success in his new undertaking."[87]

The 31-year-old new proprietor of the Mariposa Stables, Albert Henry Washburn (known around town as "Henry"), would soon play a crucial role in young George Monroe's future. Springing as would a sequoia seedling from the recent fire, Washburn's new venture would eventually provide the backdrop for George's rise to international recognition.[88]

Back in 1856, around the time that nine-year-old George Monroe was traveling from Washington, D.C. to Mariposa, two of Henry Washburn's brothers, Seth and Ed were running a general store in the nearby mining village of Bridgeport. By 1859, Henry had joined Ed in Bridgeport, just as their ailing brother Seth headed back to the family home in Putney, Vermont, where he died the following year of stomach cancer. Ed likewise returned home to Putney probably in 1864, leaving Henry on his own.[89]

In December 1865, Henry married local poet Jean Lindsay Bruce. Her nephew, John Bruce, had recently sold his interest in a Mariposa livery stable and joined Henry in a mining venture. A few months into 1866, with the Bruce & Washburn mine reporting a modest yield of $20 per ton, the partners entered into a lease of the Eureka Mine. Employing a force of skilled Chinese mine workers, the operation promised a return of $25 to $50 per ton. But the next year found Henry redirecting his prospecting efforts toward the fledgling industry of Yosemite tourism when he purchased Col. Terry's livery stable.[90]

Albert Henry Washburn and John Bridle Bruce
(Yosemite Museum and Archives)

Washburn might have sensed it was a good time to phase out of the mining business; he would have seen what had also been observed that year by a New York Times journalist:

" … here, in Mariposa County … affairs are in a desperate condition. There are in all ten quartz-mills here, all, or nearly all, on the Fremont estate, but only two or three are now running, and these with moderate results. The villages are decreasing in population; the best people are going away; viciousness of all sorts seems to be increasing, and highway robberies are of almost nightly occurrence. … The ore now being obtained and thus washed returns from $7 to $10 a ton, which gives a small margin of profit."[91]

In contrast to the lagging economy in Mariposa, the same article reports on mines far to the north:

"There are now about twenty quartz mills in successful operation in Grass Valley, and the ore they work yields from $10 to $50 a ton; occasionally as high as $100 and $200. The cost of mining and working is from $6 to $10 a ton, depending on the facilities of mine and mill."

The Bruce & Washburn Mine's yield of $20 per ton, minus costs, left little more than a small margin of profit, and their lease of the Eureka Mine may not have been living up to expectations. Henry's choice for a new business would turn out to be far more prosperous. The newly-protected Yosemite Valley and Mariposa Grove were drawing increasing attention, and Washburn may have sensed that tourism could supplant mining as a driving force of Mariposa's economy.

Washburn's new ad retained his predecessor's text, changing only the business name (from "Mariposa Stables") and that of the proprietor:

January 19, 1867[92]

Washburn's name-change from "Mariposa Stables" to Yo Semite Stables" caused a bit of a kerfuffle, leading to yet another name-change just fourteen days later. A few blocks away, John R. McCready had been running a livery stable for six years. After all that time he was still calling his place the "New Livery Stable," and had finally decided to change the name to "Yo Semite Stables." But Washburn, possibly unaware of McCready's intentions, had already published the same name for his own business in the local paper. So, in the January 19th issue of the *Gazette*, one finds not only Washburn's new ad for "Yo Semite Stables," but McCready's lingering old ad for his "New Livery Stable," as well as the now obsolete ad for Col. Terry's "Mariposa Stables" that had been bought and renamed by Washburn.

McCready likely marched into the *Gazette* office to complain that he'd come up with "Yo Semite Stables" before Washburn did, and the conflict was resolved two weeks later. On the second of February, the *Gazette* ran Washburn's newly altered ad for the "Mammoth Tree Livery Stables," and just below it, McCready's newly renamed "Yo Semite Stables." Only two years later, Washburn and McCready would become business partners.

John Jay Cook (Courtesy Tom Phillips)

The next month, John Jay Cook partnered with Washburn. Cook, a successful businessman who was married to Washburn's wife's sister, owned a drug store in Mariposa and had the capital to invest. Over the next three decades, Cook and other investors would seek to profit from Washburn's energy and business savvy. A year later Washburn's nephew and former mining partner, John Bruce, joined the business. A succession of advertisements tracks Washburn's expanding familial partnerships:

MAMMOTH TREE LIVERY
STABLES.

Corner of Bullion and 7th Streets.

A. H. WASHBURN.....................Proprietor.

February 2, 1867[93]

MAMMOTH TREE LIVERY
STABLES.

Corner of Bullion and 7th Streets.

WASHBURN & COOK....................Proprietors.

March 16, 1867[94]

MAMMOTH TREE LIVERY
STABLES.
MAIN STREET.

WASHBURN, COOK & BRUCE..........Proprietors.

March 13, 1868[95]

It is around this time that George Monroe is reported to have been employed by Washburn. Henry Washburn and German immigrant Herman Schlageter were likely old friends, said to have shared a cabin during their younger years. A corner of Schlageter's Hotel was occupied by Louis Monroe's tonsorial parlor, so there's a good chance that Monroe was Washburn's barber. Amid the lively ambiance of Schlageter's "commodious barroom" amid the scent of bay rum and tobacco smoke, Louis might have been applying final touches to Washburn's beard while apprising him of young George's special talent for horses. Or it may be that George was already making a name for himself, perhaps helping out at local livery stables. According to a later article:

" … [George Monroe] entered the employment of A. H. WASHBURN & CO., as a Yo Semite guide in 1866. In 1868 he commenced driving stage for the same company …."[96]

It is more likely that Monroe was hired by Washburn in 1867. Washburn doesn't appear to have entered the Yosemite tourism business until that year, and though he ran "carriages and buggies," Monroe would have to wait until 1869 for Washburn to start running stages.

In his first job as a guide for Washburn & Cook, George Monroe was one of at least four employees who would carry travelers by carriage and then by saddle-train through Yosemite and the Mariposa Grove. Monroe's fellow guides in 1867 were named in the *Mariposa Mail*: J. H. Wilmer, James Ridgway, and a man identified only as "Parteta." From scant data such as this, and occasional reports of vehicles used or purchased by the company, it would appear that Washburn and Cook may have started out with fewer than a dozen wagons of various description, and perhaps half that many drivers or guides. These numbers would, of course, increase with demand. By the early 1880s, there were about twenty stage drivers mentioned by name in various sources as working for Washburn and company, and by the end of the century, it was reported that in some years Washburn had as many as fifty regular drivers.[97]

During his first years of employment, George Monroe would have ample opportunity to develop his skills, spending hours training and tending the horses at the stables, and out on the trails and roads driving carriages and leading saddle-trains. Having a full-time job, he would be seeing less of his parents, who were busy making plans for their own future. Washburn, too, was making plans that would keep George busily engaged for years to come.

By April 1869, the new partnership of Washburn & McCready owned three livery stables in Mariposa. That year, Cook and Bruce are no longer listed as Washburn's partners. Cook still ran his drugstores in Mariposa and San Francisco, the latter location being where in 1874 he would also serve as a travel agent for Washburn & McCready. Bruce reappears as Washburn's partner by 1877.[98]

As Washburn was growing his business, Louis and Mary Monroe were pursuing their dream of property ownership. July 1868 brought the ratification of the Fourteenth Amendment to the United States Constitution, which cemented and expanded the rights of citizenship for African Americans without interference from individual states. At this point, any questions about the Monroes' right to homestead seem to have been resolved, and within two years they would be land owners. It was also around this time that they would have received word of the death of Mary's mother, Polly Millen, though exactly when or where she died remains unknown.[99]

Louis Monroe, as an agent for *The Elevator* newspaper, was sharing copies with the local press as evidenced by a letter from the *Mariposa Mail* to *The Elevator* in 1868:

TABLE OF ALTITUDES AT YOSEMITE VALLEY. **87/3**

WATERFALLS.

INDIAN NAME.	SIGNIFICATION.	AMERICAN NAME.	HEIGHT.
		Cataract	900 feet
Po-ho-no	Night Wind	Bridal Veil	630 feet
Yo-Semite	Large Grizzly Bear		2,634 feet
First Fall 1,600 feet ; Second Fall, 600 feet ; Third Fall, 434 feet.			
Py-wy-ack	Sparkling Water	Vernal	350 feet
Yo-wi-ye		Nevada	700 feet
Illilouette	The Beautiful	South Fork	600 feet
Yo-coy-ae	Shade to Indian Baby Basket	Royal Arch Falls	1,000 feet
Loya		Sentinel Falls	3,000 feet

MOUNTAINS.

Poo-see-nah Chuck-ka	Large Acorn Cache	Cathedral Rocks	2,660 feet
Tu-tock-a-mu-la	Great Chief of the Valley	El Capitan	3,300 feet
		The Cathedral Spires	1,800 feet
Pom-pom-pasus	Mountains Playing Leap.frog.	Three Brothers	3,830 feet
Hep-se-tuck-a-nah	Gone in	Union Rocks	3,500 feet
Loya	Signal Station	Sentinel Rock	3,043 feet
Loya	Signal Station	Sentinel Dome	4,500 feet
Ummo	Lost Arrow		3,000 feet
Patillima		Glacier Rock	3,200 feet
To-coy-ae	Shade to Indian Baby Basket	Royal Arches	1,800 feet
Hunto	The Watching Eye	Washington Column	1,875 feet
		North Dome	3,568 feet
Tis-sa-ack	Goddess of the Valley	South Dome	4,727 feet
Wayan	Pine Mountain	Mount Watkins	3,900 feet
Cloud's Rest, 6,034 feet ; Cap of Liberty, 4,000 feet ; Mt. Starr King, 5,600 feet.			

Trade Card, front and back, c. 1869, Washburn and McCready. (Yosemite
Museum & Archives)

70

"[To] The Elevator.—We are under obligations to L. A. Monroe, agent at this place, for several numbers of the San Francisco Elevator, the organ of the colored people of the Pacific Coast. We find it an able and dignified journal, earnestly and efficiently laboring for the intellectual, moral, religious and material advancement of that people. We comment it to the encouragement and support of every friend of the black man.—*Mariposa Mail.*"[100]

In 1870, the *Gazette* reported a surge of Yosemite-bound tourists through Mariposa—400 travelers in 25 days from May 13 to June 14.[101] Around this time, certainly by the following spring, Washburn and McCready were well into the tourist stage business:

Eleven-passenger stage in the Mariposa Grove ca. 1900. Signs visible on the front three sequoias left to right read: "Georgia," "Stonewall Jackson," "Robert E. Lee" (Courtesy Jeff Henderson Collection)

"New Stage.—Washburn & McCready, who are running a daily line of stages between Mariposa and Clark & Moore's, where they connect with their saddle train for Yo Semite, received on Saturday last a splendid eleven-passenger stage,

71

which they immediately placed upon the road. It runs smooth and is just the thing for the mountains. It was made in Stockton."[102]

Clark & Moore's was the current business name for Galen Clark's rustic hotel, midway between Mariposa and Yosemite Valley. At the end of the 1860s, Clark & Moore's employed an African American named George McEwen, whose brief exchange with a foreign tourist drew notice in the local *Mariposa Mail*:

"George McEwen is also there [at Clark's], assisting everybody in his usual quiet and gentlemanly manner. George was rather taken aback the other day, when a long gander-legged Dutchman, on a tour of the Valley, and eager to receive every attention without regard to the convenience of others, stepped up to George and demanded to know where his *master waz*. Cooly surveying the imperious individual a minute or so, George replied: 'Don't know — haven't seen him since the war.'"[103]

The degree of respect reflected in *Gazette* coverage of the African American community around this time is notable, while at the same time their coverage of travelers, foreign and domestic, could be far less hospitable. Here's an example:[104]

" ... some of the foreign elements which were gathered [in Yosemite] during the late Sunday-school assembly, were far more curious than any produced either by nature, or, as Prof. [John] Muir asserts, by glaciers.

So many tourists go to the Valley who fondly imagine that they — not the sublimity of Yo Semite — are the points of especial interest, and as a result they throw the very unwelcome light of disgraceful egotism over themselves.

… The hotel managers and stage drivers deserve the commiseration of the entire public for their untiring patience, and when our genial friends … present themselves at St. Peter's Gate … we are sure if they mention to the sentinel that they had to entertain the Yo Semite Sunday School Assembly, he will open wide the pearly gate and motion them to the place of honor among the venerated martyrs of ages gone."

Mr. Staples and his Sabbath School; photograph by George Fiske (Yosemite Museum & Archives)

Incidentally, during the "Sunday-school assembly," the Yosemite Chapel was dedicated, John Muir gave a public lecture on "geology and rock sculpture," and attendees were treated to a concert by the famous Hutchinson Family singers.[105]

In the early 1870s, George Monroe's employers were grappling with some stiff competition, including from stage operators Samuel & Zenas Fisher & Co. This was spurred by the impending arrival of railroad tracks being laid at a furious pace down California's central valley. Soon the railroad would bring an explosion of business, and both Fisher and Washburn were coordinating with the newly formed San Joaquin Valley branch of the Central Pacific Railroad to connect Yosemite-bound travelers with their respective stage lines.

But the railroad was not the only pressing matter; there was a good deal of urgent attention being given to the development of stage roads into Yosemite. In 1870 the Fishers partnered with Clark and Moore to complete a toll stage road connecting Mariposa to Clark & Moore's. Washburn and McCready might well have been alarmed at this news; having to pay road-tolls to their competitors could permanently lock their business into second-place. At the same time, there were several other proposals for new roads to Yosemite from the north and west. Beyond that, with the promise of the coming railroad and construction of new stage roads, new tourist-guide ventures were cropping up.[106]

One of those new ventures was situated at the terminus of the Mariposa stage road, where passengers would transfer to guided saddle trains bound for Yosemite:

"New Advertisements To-day
FOR YO SEMITE VALLEY! -AND THE- Big Tree Grove!
BY THE MARIPOSA ROUTE! GORDON & RIDGWAY, THE
PIONEER GUIDES, WOULD RESPECTFULLY

ANNOUNCE TO YOSEMITE TOURISTS,
That they are prepared to
FURNISH COMPLETE OUTFITS AND THE BEST OF SADDLE
HORSES,
And to give their personal attention to the comfort and
accommodations of travelers.

... PETER GORDON, JAMES A. RIDGWAY."[107]

But out of the fog of this competitive climate, Washburn would emerge at the top. Over the ensuing years, James Ridgway, Peter Gordon (named in the above ad), and three subsequent generations of Gordons would be employed by companies run or spearheaded by Henry Washburn. And Fisher would eventually work in cooperation with Washburn & McCready.[108]

(Library of Congress Prints and Photographs Division)[109]

Chapter IV

THE ROAD TO YOSEMITE — *Monroe Ranch. Washburn builds a transportation empire. George Monroe gains stature as a stage-driver.*

In February 1870, the Fifteenth Amendment to the United States Constitution was ratified under the administration of Ulysses S. Grant, establishing that the "right of citizens of the United States to vote shall not be denied or abridged by the United States or by any state on account of race, color, or previous condition of servitude."[110]

One month later, Louis Monroe made local history:

> "Several colored citizens during the past week have placed their names on the Great Register of Mariposa county. L. A. Monroe, an old resident of this place, being the first to enter his name. Our County Clerk will place the names of all colored men, entitled to vote, on the Register when they present themselves for that purpose at his office."[111]

The famous illustration in Harper's Weekly later that year depicted the universality of this historic moment so fittingly that it could almost have been Monroe himself in the image, though he may have been better-dressed than the craftsman first in line (with a hammer in his left pocket and a patched pant-leg), more like the businessman second in line. The businessman is followed by a Union Army veteran, analogous to a Mariposa area African American veteran named Alexander Pelton. Behind him appears to be a farmer who, curiously, is looking toward a light-complexioned, possibly feminine face, perhaps included as a reminder that women, of any color, had been excluded from the legislation.

The 1870 census reveals that Mary Monroe was "Keeping house," listing the value of her real estate at $350 with Mary as the property owner. The listing also shows George living at home with his parents in or near the town of Mariposa. But by this time the Monroes were also the proud new owners of farmland, well outside of town, with Mary in charge. Having learned of a state law authorizing married women to operate their own businesses, in two years she would announce:

> "... I, MARY ANN MONROE, wife of L.A. Monroe ... shall apply ... for an order of said Court permitting me to carry on the business of farming and stock raising in my own name and on my own account, in said Township and County, as sole trader. Dated Mariposa, December 23d, 1871."[112]

Though Louis still listed his profession as "Barber," he was now experimenting with a new career. In June 1871 Louis walked into the office of the *Gazette* with a small treasure:

> "Mountain Wheat.—L. A. Monroe has left at this office this week a hand full of wheat heads which he says are about a fair sample of a field of 30 acres on his ranch a few miles from town. The heads average six inches in length, are well filled with grains generally plump, though in some of the heads the grains show the effect of deficient moisture. Monroe says the straw is from three to four feet in length. Such a crop this dry season indicates that the hill lands are most reliable and valuable wheat lands. If that is the case it is certain such lands are not utilized to one hundredth part of the extent they ought to be."[113]

So, while Louis was juggling two careers, barbering in town and then, most likely with Mary, heading out to work on developing the new ranch, George could remain in their Mariposa home while working at the Washburn & McCready stables.

Washburn & McCready were also busy showing off their energy and ingenuity, which in one instance led to a brush with history:

"Yosemite Items.— … The first carriage in the valley arrived here July 24th [1871], packed in on mules by Washburn & McCready, livery men of the Mariposa route, for the use of the public. Tourists who have an objection to horseback riding can enjoy the sights and wonders of this remarkable valley, combined with the pleasures of a carriage ride. … Mrs. [Elizabeth] Cady Stanton and Susan B. Anthony are at Yo Semite, visiting the different points of interest in Washburn & McCready's carriage, being the first to enjoy a carriage ride in Yo Semite valley."[114]

1871 finds Washburn & McCready angling to create a transportation empire. Railroad workers edged southward through central California, their freshly laid tracks bringing Yosemite tourists into closer range of Washburn & McCready's stage lines. In anticipation, the firm appears to have established a connection with the railroad to the north in Modesto, and built a stable farther south where the railroad would soon reach a settlement called Bear Creek:

"We understand that it is the intention of Washburn & McCready to erect a large livery stable this Winter at Bear Creek, and stock it with plenty of horses, carriages, stages, &c., for the accommodation of Yo Semite tourists next season. This firm has already a large amount of capital invested in this business. The above firm have recently purchased Boomershine's stage line running from Modesto to Coulterville."[115]

The newly purchased interest in the Modesto-Coulterville route brought tourists by stage from the Modesto railroad depot to Coulterville, thence on horseback to Yosemite's northern entrance on the Coulterville trail. The new Bear Creek location would connect railroad customers to a one-day stage-ride to Mariposa.[116]

Every year, as roads and trails became impassible from mud and snow, the Yosemite tourist season would gradually slow and then close down for the winter. Horses would be driven from the company's stage stations to stables at lower, warmer elevations, where George Monroe and his fellow teamsters would stay busy with training and exercising the company livestock. Other specialists would tend to the rolling stock, carpenters fashioning replacement parts, and blacksmiths forging new hardware. Skilled painters applied bright red and yellow to the stages, deftly lettering the company name on the sides along with decorative flourishes and pinstriping. More than just for decoration, scraping and painting were crucial to the maintenance of vehicles that were exposed to rain, mud, and searing sun over miles of dirt roads. Foreshadowing the title of a 1951 Broadway musical, a *Gazette* ad for the local paint dealer trumpeted "Look here! Paint your wagons."[117]

Winter was also the time to plan and develop infrastructure for the next season, and perhaps to take a vacation. Over the winter of 1871-72, while railroad track laborers advanced south into Bear Creek, Henry Washburn and his wife, Jean, visited his family in Vermont, and her family in New York. About the time the Washburns were heading east, it was being reported that Bear Creek would be renamed "Ashmore" by the Southern Pacific Railroad, even though the company's practice of naming towns for company executives and financiers had been coming under popular derision all year. A sarcastic article in January nicely summed up the issue:

"The Mariposa *Free Press* says that 'Ashmore' is proposed as the name of the future town at the terminus of the San Joaquin Valley Railroad, on Bear Creek. Ralston declined the honor of having his name affixed to what is now Modesto. We are happy to know that Colonel Nelson Ashmore has no such weakness. … The Colonel has been kind enough to give us his pedigree, from which we extract the following, in his own language: '… Look at me! I'm the most financierenst man that ever marked the yearth.' The Colonel consents to have his name bestowed upon the new town. It's a good name; has a musical sound; beats Modesto, and is ahead of Ralston."

By the time the Washburns returned home, Colonel Ashmore seems to have backed down, and the settlement of Bear Creek had been given a different new name, in honor of its home county and the nearby river that flowed from Yosemite Valley — Merced.[118]

In May, one month after the Washburns returned from the east, a milestone was achieved — now travelers could purchase a single round-trip ticket from San Francisco for their Yosemite vacation:

"Yo Semite Travel — New Arrangement. — Washburn & McCready advertise to take passengers through from San Francisco to the Yo Semite Valley and back for $55. The trip includes in its rounds the Big Tree Grove. They connect with Fisher & Co., at Mariposa. Tickets can be procured at the office of the Central Pacific Railroad. Saddle animals are furnished at the South Fork [Clark & Moore's] for the trip to the Trees and Valley without extra charge ...."[119]

Ca. 1872 Central Pacific R.R. engine at El Capitan Hotel, Merced (Courtesy Milt Harker)

In 1871 the *Gazette* reprinted news about the increasing number of Black voters in San Francisco, probably from Louis Monroe's copy of *The Elevator*:

> "The Colored Vote. — The editor of the *Elevator* newspaper, an organ of the colored people in San Francisco, thinks their vote will exceed 2,500, and may go as high as 3,000."[120]

The next year, George Monroe joined their ranks as a registered voter, giving his occupation as "teamster." At the same time, the voter rolls show his father identifying himself no longer as a barber, but as a "rancher."[121] In 1873 we're given a description of the Monroe property in the Delinquent Tax List, published in the *Mariposa Gazette*. "Monroe, Mrs. L. A." is shown as owning 160 acres "about six miles from Mariposa, on road from Mormon Bar to Kehoe & Mailons' [*sic*] old ranch, valued at $200" with $300 in improvements. It also itemizes their possessions:

"One wagon $50; farming utensils $20; six horses $180; two colts $10; one cow $30; one calf $5; three stock cattle $45; thirty hogs $100; crop $200; furniture $25; twelve chickens $4; firearms $15; amount of assessment $1,184; tax $34.80."[122]

Louis' and Mary's efforts at developing and running their farm were paying off, and they did eventually pay their taxes. Meanwhile, George's employment kept him away from the farm most of the time. It is of more than passing interest that George Monroe appears in a *Gazette* blurb in April 1874, giving his address as Merced, California:

"Arrivals at the Mariposa Hotel … Tuesday, April 14 … George F. Monroe, Merced."[123]

Washburn and McCready may have been putting their best on the front line by posting Monroe in Merced. There Monroe, a talented driver now with seven years' experience with the company, would be positioned to receive travelers at the El Capitan Hotel, refreshed from their overnight train ride and fully breakfasted, and deliver them to their evening's waystation along the Coulterville Road. Others taking the Mariposa route would board one of Fisher's stages at 7 a.m. and arrive in Mariposa by 4 p.m., where they would transfer to a Washburn & McCready stage to Clark and Moore's, and then ride horseback via saddle trains to Yosemite.[124]

Though his address was given as Merced by the newspaper, the mobile nature of George's occupation makes it hard to pin down just where he called home. His voter registrations continue to name Mariposa as his primary residence through 1875, then the next year he gives his home as Merced, and finally Yosemite

(Valley) in 1879. But wherever the end of the day's route happened to be, George could expect a barn for the horses, the company of his fellow drivers, a meal, and a bunkhouse in which to spend the night, all provided through his employment.[125]

In 1872 *New York Times* journalist Sara Jane Lippincott gave a colorful, detailed description of her trip through Merced to Clark & Moore's, taking the Fisher stage to Mariposa and connecting to the Washburn & McCready stage line. Lippincott (better known by her pseudonym Grace Greenwood) and her party of seven took the train from San Francisco to Merced on June the fourth. There she described checking in to the "elegant new hotel, El Capitan" where "things were in rather an unsettled, unfinished state." That evening they were kept awake by a noisy party of young revelers: "To their ordinary nocturnal diversions of dancing, singing, laughing, and whistling, they occasionally added the unparalleled atrocity of the accordion." George Monroe may have heard the ruckus while trying to sleep before his next run via the Coulterville Road. Of the trip to Mariposa, Lippincott wrote:

"The stage-ride from Merced over the plain to the foot-hills was not tedious, for the road led through magnificent golden grain-fields, ready for harvest; but we were not sorry to reach the rising ground and the shade of woods. Hornitos was our dining-place,—a place to be remembered for its nice hotel and nicer landlady. The drive from this point to Mariposa is quite delightful …. At Mariposa we were obliged to wait, with another party of tourists, some five hours, till coaches should come down from White and Hatch's …. The little old mining town, so long associated with the fame and fortunes of General Frémont, has now but a dismal and dilapidated look, though it is said business is reviving there somewhat."

Why the Lippincott party was obliged to wait in Mariposa could be that they had already booked the option, offered by the Washburn & McCready stage line, to continue the extra twelve miles to White and Hatch's hotel. But the five-hour wait suggests that there had been a scheduling error, or that all the Mariposa hotels were at capacity, forcing a last-minute change of accommodations.

While waiting for the stages to arrive, Lippincott decided to pass the time by attending a local minstrel show, which was prefaced by an impromptu political rally as the gathering audience waited for the performers to start. Among the spectators, Lippincott observed miners, drovers, a Native American, a Chinese man, a Mexican mule-driver, several small boys, and eight "small girls in their Sunday best." Nonetheless, she reported that "a happy unanimity seemed to prevail in our meeting." Various travelers and locals stood and gave orations on opposing sides of the political spectrum. Of the minstrels, she wrote, "Every role was duly filled; there was the aggravating conundrum-man, and the proper end-man, and the funny end-man, who played on the tambourine with his knees and his heels and his nose, and banged it against his head ...."[126]

Finally, the stage arrived: "We had a rather anxious night-ride of twelve miles, over a rough road, through streams and gullies, and along steep, rocky canyons, to the hotel of White and Hatch, which we did not reach till one o'clock in the morning." After breakfast the next morning they continued by stage:

" ... to the end of the stage-road, the famous ranch of Clark and Moore, on the South Merced,—a lovely, lonely, piny, primitive place, with a peculiarly peaceful, restful atmosphere pervading it. Here we were received with simple, hearty cordiality ...."

One woman rides astride, while the other two are on sidesaddles. Clark and Moore's is in the background; Galen Clark is seated on the log at left.

(Yosemite Museum and Archives)[127]

Preparing the next morning for a horseback-ride up to the Mariposa Grove, Lippincott's party discovered that all the horses with sidesaddles had been pre-booked by another group, "and that we must tarry there indefinitely, or take to the Mexican saddle," that is, astride. Lippincott, an outspoken advocate for women's suffrage and equal pay, not to mention the abolition of slavery in pre-emancipation days, was equally candid with her views on the subject of riding sidesaddle:

"So, with a tear for the modest traditions of our sex, and a shudder at the thought of the figures we should present, we four brave women accepted the situation, and, for the nonce, rode as woman used to ride in her happy, heroic days, before Satan, for her entanglement and enslavement, invented trained skirts, corsets, and side-saddles. ... We all came to the conclusion that this style of riding is the safest, easiest, and therefore the most sensible, for long mountain expeditions, and for steep, rough, and narrow trails. If Nature intended woman to ride horseback at all, she doubtless intended it should be after this fashion, otherwise we should have been a sort of land variety of the mermaid."

After a day at the Mariposa Grove, she describes the summer evening's entertainment at Clark and Moore's:

"Though the days were warm in that charming resting-place, beside the unresting Merced, the nights were very cool; and a bright camp-fire in front of the hotel was surrounded till a late hour by a circle of tourists, guides, pack-mule men, and stage-drivers. We took to reciting ballads and telling stories. Of the latter, the most horrible and hair-elevating sort were at a premium.

... Early the next morning we were mounted and away, eager for the Yosemite, yet reluctantly taking leave of our hosts, Clark and Moore, both very interesting men, mountaineers of the best type,—and their kindly household.

... As we jogged along, single file, we formed an odd, but not a very picturesque procession .... We found our guide— Peter Gordon, at your service! a remarkably agreeable young man—modest, but not averse to imparting information."[128]

For three years, Washburn & McCready had been steadily expanding their business, purchasing horses and adding new stages to their rolling stock. Back in June 1871, the *Gazette* reported:

"Still the tide of Yo Semite travel flows strongly and steadily. From one to five stages and carriages daily arrive loaded with passengers; even the 'hurricane deck' of the stages being often crowded.

Washburn & McCready are constantly training and exercising teams, so as to be prepared to meet any increased demand that may be made on them.

Over 80 tourists were ticketed to Yo Semite on Monday last in San Francisco, and it is said that many are holding back for the rush to subside, though they fear they shall lose something by doing so through a diminution of the volume of water at the falls.

There need be no alarm on that score. There was much snow in the mountains last Winter; the season has been uncommonly cool hitherto; and there will be plenty of water for two months to come. Besides, tourists who will go to Glacier Point, if only for an hour or two, will see that the most magnificent feature of the Valley is not liable to dry up at any season, till 'the heavens shall be rolled together as a scroll.'"[129]

But now Washburn & McCready had to work fast. In 1874 two new routes under construction, the Big Oak Flat Road and the Coulterville Road, would soon bring tourist stages from the north clear into Yosemite Valley, and threaten to bring the promising Mariposa tourist industry to its knees. The current practice of transferring from stages to saddle-trains at Clark & Moore's was soon to be rendered obsolete. The only way to compete with the northern routes would be to build a new road from Clark & Moore's so stages could continue all the way into Yosemite Valley.

The partners also had a new threat on their own turf. For two years they had worked in cooperation with the stage-line of Fisher & Company, but with the untimely death of Samuel Fisher from a runaway stage accident, his firm was being sold, and the new owners intended to compete with Washburn & McCready. To add to their difficulties, McCready had been in failing health for the past few months, obliging Washburn to assume an ever-increasing role in their partnership.[130]

Amid the swirling competition, with their stages already in operation between Merced and Coulterville, Washburn & McCready were strategically positioned to roll into Yosemite the very instant that the Coulterville Road opened on June 18. George Monroe is said to have been the driver of the first stage on the route.

Washburn & McCready launched a new advertisement for stages from Merced to Yosemite Valley on the new road:

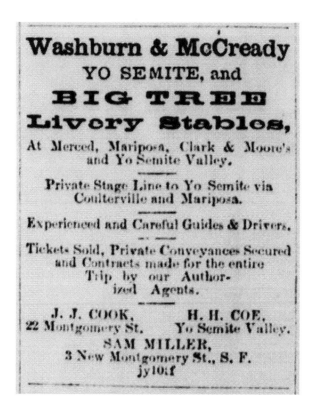

ISSUED BY WASHBURN & McCREADY.

GOOD FOR ONE PASSAGE FROM

YOSEMITE
TO
MERCED.

Via either Coulterville or Inspiration P't Routes.

If holder uses this via Mariposa and lays over—or makes a break in the continuous passage between Yosemite and Clarks—an extra charge will be collected by the guide for such extra time and use of saddle horse.

Yosemite and Return. } **Washburn & McCready.**

This does not include use of Horses, Guides, or Toll in Valley. Takes parties only to and from Hotel.

405

CHECK

Trade Card stamped June 7, 1874, two weeks before the opening of the Coulterville Road (Courtesy John Carpenter Collection)

But as this new phase of Yosemite tourism was getting underway, McCready's health started to decline so rapidly that he turned his attention from the stage-business to preparing his will. That August he suffered a "violent attack of hemorrhage" while traveling by stage to Clark & Moore's and died two weeks later. Grieving the loss of his partner, Washburn pressed forward. Gathering the support of friends and investors, Washburn's efforts would effectively save the local economy by preserving the Mariposa tourist industry. Within the space of a single year, Washburn would acquire the strategically placed Clark & Moore's hotel, and construct the crucially needed new road into Yosemite Valley.[131]

About two months before the December 22, 1874 purchase of Clark & Moore's, Washburn and two new partners, E. W. Chapman and W. F. Coffman, contracted with Clark's partner Edwin Moore and roadbuilder John Conway to build the new wagon-road into Yosemite Valley.[132] On the second of November 1874, even as Washburn was in the process of applying for a road permit, an improved bridge over the South Fork Merced River, stout enough to support loaded stages and freight wagons, was already under construction:

"A. H. Washburn and E. W. Chapman, through their attorney, L. F. Jones, make application asking that the Board [of Supervisors] appoint two commissioners to act in conjunction with the surveyor of the applicants and a commissioner appointed by them, to lay out a toll wagon road beginning at or near the northerly end of the bridge across the South Fork of the Merced River at Clark & Moore's ranch, known as Clark's bridge, now in process of construction—thence in a generally easterly direction to the boundary line of Yo Semite Grant, and wholly within Mariposa county ...."[133]

Eadweard Muybridge, "Merced River At Clark & Moore's" 1872. Shows Clark's bridge, constructed in 1868 (Courtesy Dennis Kruska)[134]

Wawona Covered Bridge, an 1874 rebuild of Clark's 1868 bridge, photographed in about 1920 (Yosemite Museum and Archives)

The Wawona Covered Bridge functions to this day. Under the direction of Conway, skilled Chinese roadbuilders worked through the rainy winter of 1875, and by April, Washburn was already running stages along the partially completed route.

Washburn had renamed Clark & Moore's, calling it Big Tree Station, and the new route into Yosemite Valley would be called the Mariposa Road:[135]

> "Tourists.—The yearly travel to the Yo Semite Valley has now fairly set in. Washburn, Chapman & Co. are running a daily line of stages on their route, which lies through Hornitos, Princeton, Mariposa and Big Tree Station to the Hermitage; thence into the Valley. Nearly two hundred men are now at work on the Yo Semite end of this road. On and after May 1st there will be but four miles of horseback travel on this route, which will be daily and as rapidly decreased as two hundred laborers can do it."[136]

A grand opening ceremony for the completed road took place on July 22nd.

The "Hermitage" (mentioned in the above quote) was a point of curiosity for travelers. Located along the horse-trail near the south-western entrance to Yosemite Valley, high above the valley floor, it was described by John Erastus Lester in 1873:

> "As you come down the Mariposa trail … you pass a large tree, around the trunk of which you see some rough boards standing with inclined sides. You examine the rude structure and find that the boards cover a great opening in the tree which fire had made and that the space within scarcely allows a man to lie with extended limbs. Your guide tells you that the hermit lived here and that he died in the valley and is buried near the banks of the swift flowing Merced."

According to Lester, Yosemite resident James Lamon identified the hermit as James or Henry Wilmer of New York who, in Lamon's words, "shew his good bringing up, and I think he was born a gentleman" and "sought in the great mountain solitude escape from his cares." According to Lamon, "Poor Wilmer" became "more and more dejected and sad" about "terrible and unrelenting adversities and domestic troubles coming upon him" apparently reported through letters sent to him from his native New York, and "had fully resolved to take his own life." Lamon found Wilmer's body on the bank of the Merced River and buried him nearby.[137]

Opening of the Mariposa Road, Henry Washburn appears to be seated at left, presumably alongside Chapman and Coffman (Yosemite Museum and Archives)

Four-horse stage on the Wawona Road
(Yosemite Museum and Archives)

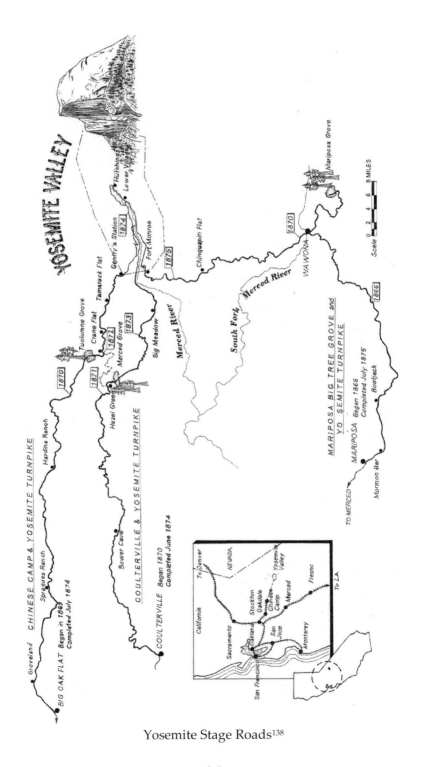

Yosemite Stage Roads[138]

Chapter V

CELEBRITY — *George Monroe's famous passengers.*
Washburn grows his business while George's parents perfect
the Monroe Ranch.

George Monroe was likely on hand to drive stages through the covered bridge and over the new road, as the *Gazette* reports that while in the vicinity of Big Tree Station (now Wawona), he was pressed into service to help capture a local thief. The article also indicates that at least sixty Chinese roadbuilders were still employed at the end of June 1875:

"Robbery. — On Friday night last a Chinaman blacksmith in the employ of the Chinese company on the Washburn, Chapman & Co road, committed a robbery by taking the money the paymaster had in charge to pay the hands. It was in a box, and supposed to contain from twelve to fifteen hundred dollars. The morning after the theft was discovered, the box was found on the premises broken open, the contents gone, and an ax near by. Notice was immediately given, and Deputy Sheriff West went up with a warrant on Monday to look into the matter. After learning all he could in relation to it, he availed himself of the services of Al Sleeper, John L. Murphy, Ralf Gallison, James A. Ridgway, Geo. Monroe, Geo. Temple and Ceneral Partida, he took position at the bridge near Big Tree Station, and in the course of the day went through about fifty Chinamen. That night Ralph Gallison and West guarded the bridge, and about 11 o'clock the next day they searched ten more, and a short time afterward along came the aforesaid blacksmith, with his blankets and a pistol. He was told to throw down his bundle and pistol and submit to a search. He appeared obstinate, but the leveled six-shooters operated as persuaders. A rich deposit revealed itself, $815.25 in gold being found secreted in his bundle. The whole amount stolen was not found upon him, $200 in gold and $200 in gold notes. He was conducted to town and lodged in jail. Deputy Sheriff West performed this job well."[139]

Monroe's reassignment to include the new Yosemite route was no small matter, as it would involve relocating not only Monroe but his several teams of horses. Stages would stop multiple times along the road to change horses at strategically placed barns. Later maps indicate that there would be five stage stops between Wawona and Yosemite Valley. Drivers such as Monroe each had their own horses that were accustomed to their driver's voice, commands, personality, and even their scent. At the time it was typical that six horses were used per stage, meaning that each driver could have had as many as thirty or more personally trained horses distributed along the Wawona-Yosemite route. In a six-horse configuration, the front pair of horses called the "leader team," would be most critical in understanding the driver's commands; the "swing team"—the two middle horses—added power in cornering, while the "wheel team" closest to the stage would do most of the pulling, even helping in steering the vehicle.[140]

The new route would have George spending his nights away from home in one of the bunkhouses maintained by the stage company. He changed his official primary residence from Mariposa to Merced in 1876, possibly indicating that his parents had finally sold their Mariposa home, as they'd been living on their ranch for several years. Merced also was one of the locations where the stage company wintered their horses, and Monroe would have been on hand to train and exercise the stage stock.[141]

Six-horse stage on the Wawona Road, photo by George Fiske. A hand-written caption identifies the driver as Uriah Toby
(Yosemite Museum and Archives)

Men's Bunkhouse, for the use of stage drivers and other employees. This one was located above the east bank of the South Fork of the Merced River, a little upstream from the Wawona Covered Bridge
(Yosemite Museum and Archives)

1876 was probably the year that Washburn & Bruce engaged 40-year-old Joseph Shelly, an Ohioan from the Sherlock Creek area of Mariposa, to construct a new 16-room hotel building just to the south-east of Clark's original rustic lodgings. Shelly family tradition has it that Joseph had also designed and built the Wawona Covered Bridge, two years earlier. The new structure dubbed the "Long White," would provide accommodations at a level more suitable to the clientele Washburn and Bruce sought to please.[142]

With George settled into his new stage route, daily carrying rapturous sightseers through stunningly beautiful forests into the incomparable Yosemite, his parents devoted their days to hard work on the ranch at Pea Ridge, farming the wheat field, tending their stock of hogs, cows, chickens and horses, and building and maintaining fences, barns, outbuildings, and their own home. Though working at home as a rancher, Louis Monroe regularly commuted six-miles by horseback or carriage to his barber shop in Mariposa. The *Gazette* noted that he changed his business location in 1877, joining the popular saloonkeeper Joseph Miller at his Capital Saloon, one door north of the north-west corner of 5th Street and Main:

"NEW BARBER SHOP,
At J. H. Miller's Saloon, MARIPOSA.
L. A. MONROE.........Prop.
SHAVING AND HAIR CUTTING
Done with dispatch, and in the most approved style."[143]

George's employer pressed forward in building his business, attracting and rewarding his investors. In March of that year, Henry Washburn bought out his partners' half-ownership of Big Tree Station, including the stage road that linked the hotel with the Mariposa area, for $20,000. Washburn was named on the deed as

100

the sole owner of the properties, though he had continued to attract investors:

> "Behind Change.—A change has taken place in the business firm of Messrs. Washburn, Chapman & Co., heretofore doing a livery business in this place and Merced, and proprietors of the Merced and Yo Semite Valley Stage Line. Messrs Chapman and Coffman retiring from the firm and Mr J. J. Cook, of San Francisco, and John B. Bruce of Merced having purchased their interests. The business will hereafter be carried on by these gentlemen in connection with Mr. A. H. Washburn."[144]

Cook sold his drug store in Mariposa and once again invested in Washburn's promising career. Washburn's nephew John Bruce was back on board, too, with his name proudly emblazoned in the ads for "Washburn & Bruce's Upper Livery Stable" at Charles St. and 6th. Though Cook's name disappeared from "Washburn & Bruce" advertisements later that March, he remained an investor, and became a board member when Washburn and various partners incorporated the Yosemite Stage & Turnpike Company near the end of 1877.[145]

In 1878, poet and renowned Civil War correspondent Benjamin Franklin Taylor left vivid impressions of traveling by stage with George Monroe at the reins. Taylor's account leaves tiny disconnected clues to how the stage company scheduled its drivers: Monroe carries Taylor only from the vicinity of Cold Springs into Big Tree Station (a distance of about ten miles) where Taylor disembarks, while Monroe likely continues to Yosemite Valley, perhaps with his remaining passengers and taking on additional travelers from the hotel. For the next day, Monroe's movements aren't documented, and Taylor takes a daylong horseback ride to visit the Mariposa Grove. The following day a driver named Mott carries Taylor from Big Tree Station to Inspiration Point, where his party is met by a stage coming up from Yosemite Valley driven by Monroe. Monroe then swings his stage around and loads Taylor and his fellow travelers for the short jaunt back into the valley. Of the first leg of the trip from Cold Springs, Taylor writes:

> "We met the out-coming stage and exchanged drivers, taking George Monroe—everybody's George—a capital fellow and a born reinsman, for our Jehu. We halted at a watering-place for man and beast, called Cold Spring, where, under a dingy veranda, sat and stood as motley a group as ever wore clothes. Grizzly men under worn-out straw bee-hives of hats … thin-flanked hunters in belt, knife and rifle; dogs dozing about, working their mouths in dreams of barking that never came true; shaggy ponies and hammer-headed horses that drooped alike at both ends. There was no premium on dirt in the crowd. It was too plenty. Not one of them spoke a word while the stage remained, but just watched us. … You could feel their silent eyes sliding all over you like drops of cold rain trickling down your back. They might have been harmless as doves, but I was privately glad when George swung himself up to the box, whirled his whip from the top of the coach with a pistol-shot at the end of it, and away we went like the king's couriers.
>
> After a succession of ups and downs, we came at last to the *descensus Averni* of the journey, and George made it *facilis*. When we struck the summit and rolled over the verge—have you ever shot the rapids of the St. Lawrence? — well, when we went over the dam, that whip began to fire platoons, and

those four horses hollowed their backs and their ears blew flat upon their necks, and we met the great pines and redwoods going up the mountain as if bound to storm something on the top of it. George talked to the four-in-hand one after another, to the tune of "get out of the way, you are all unlucky," and that is it to a minim. That team couldn't run away. It had all it could do to keep the road clear, for the stage went of itself. Wheels, axles, chains, bolts, rattled like a fanning-mill in a fever. The chaff of dust flew out behind us as if we were kicking the mountain to atoms, the curtains blew out like wings. We all sat still as mice.

... Most mountains have elbows, some of them like Briareus, a hundred, and they hold their arms akimbo like a nervous woman with a big washing. The mantel-shelves of roads are built along the edges of these arms out to the angle zig! in to the shoulder zag! There were about fifty elbows to that grade, and the horses made for every one of them at a dead run, as if the centrifugal force had got away with them. They struck "the crazy-bone" and George reined them in just in time—it was crazy-bone pretty much all the way—and then shot into the pocket of the arm-pit like a billiard ball. First you wince to the right and then to the left, as the stage swings and sways. Given an old-fashioned rail fence \/\/\/\/\/ built straight up a hill, at an angle of about forty degrees, and then scare a red squirrel down the top rails from the summit to the bottom, and you will know how we went. But we reached the last pocket as safely as if we had been so many young kangaroos in the maternal pouch, and we had made the five-mile run, and taken the chances, in twenty minutes, which is a geometrical tumble of five miles endwise at the rate of fifteen miles an hour." [146]

Stage road between Inspiration Point and Bridal Veil Fall[147]

Taylor rejoined Monroe for the famously steep grade from Inspiration Point down toward Bridal Veil Fall and Yosemite Valley. Remembering Monroe's intense stage ride from two days previous, Taylor beseeched:

> "Let us down easy, George," for our old driver was going back with the coach. He generally untied the double-bows of the road "by the run," but he just walked the horses every foot of the way, and spelled down the Z's like an urchin laboring through a hard word by the help of a schoolma'am's index finger. It was easy as swinging down in a basket, but it was not heroic."[148]

Through the mid-'70s, Washburn was assigning George Monroe to carry high-profile travelers into Big Tree Station and Yosemite Valley. Monroe must have developed his talents to a considerable level, not only as an expert stage driver but as a tourist guide interacting with an often highly elite company of international travelers. Journalist Ben C. Truman, who wrote about Monroe in a couple of articles from 1898 and 1903, observed, "Probably no man, living or dead, has ever driven so many illustrious people" including Presidents, Senators, Congressmen, eminent journalists, and artists. Truman provided a sample of luminaries to whom Monroe introduced the wonders of Yosemite:[149]

Political figures

The 18th, 19th, and 20th U. S. Presidents, respectively: Ulysses S. Grant, Rutherford B. Hayes, and James A. Garfield
William T. Sherman, General of the Union Army in the American Civil War

James G. Blaine, Congressman and later Senator from Maine (he lost his presidential bid by a narrow margin to Grover Cleveland)

Senators William M. Stewart (Nevada) and John Tyler Morgan (Alabama)

John Russell Young, journalist, author, diplomat, and Librarian of the United States Congress. Young accompanied U.S. Grant to document his two-year world tour

Other famous journalists

George Augustus Sala, English author, and journalist (wrote a travelogue of North America); Charles Anderson Dana (author, senior government official, and friend of Ulysses S. Grant); Carl Schurz (German revolutionary, American statesman); William Howard "Bull Run" Russell (Irish war correspondent); George Alfred Townsend (war correspondent); Charles Nordhoff (German-American journalist)

Royalty, Aristocracy, Gentry, Society

Princess Louise, Duchess of Argyll, Louisa Caroline Alberta, 4th daughter of Queen Victoria.

The Duke of Cumberland, aka Prince Ernest Augustus, Crown Prince of Hanover

Marquis of Salisbury, aka Robert Arthur Talbot Gascoyne-Cecil, 3rd Marquess of Salisbury. He was the British Prime Minister three times for a total of over thirteen years

Lady Franklin, aka Jane Franklin, second wife of the English explorer Sir John Franklin

Sir Arthur Sullivan, English composer of "The Lost Chord" and "Onward Christian Soldiers" as well as many operettas (with W. S. Gilbert)

Lillie Langtry, aka Emilie Charlotte Langtry, British-American socialite, actress, and producer

Artists

Albert Bierstadt, German-American painter

Thomas Moran, American painter

Thomas Hill, American painter

Charles Dorman Robinson, American painter

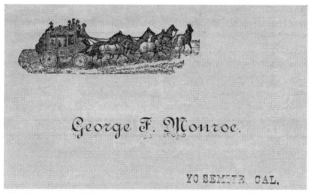

Calling card (Courtesy John Carpenter collection)[150]

Truman gave this description of Monroe:

"His dress was a combination of Old Mexican and the newest American adaptation; his hat a creamy-white, half-stiff, half-limp ....

He never had an accident; always made time, either way, to a minute; knew every peak and tree and rock and canon and clearing and hut and streamlet by the wayside. He was of medium stature, and weighed 165 pounds; he dressed neatly and wore the whitest and handsomest gauntlets of any driver in the Sierra. He was of a melancholy nature, oft times driving the entire distance from Wawona to Inspiration Point without uttering a word or relaxing a feature. But if he had a jolly crowd behind, he would watch his team carefully and listen radiantly to the jokes, stories, conundrums, and conversation, of those in his charge."

Truman then quotes Henry Washburn, who praises Monroe as having risen to the top among his many peers:

"After an experience of nearly forty years, and having had as many as fifty regular drivers some seasons, I have never known another such an all-round reinsman as George Monroe. Just as there are the greatest of soldiers and sailors, artists and mechanics at times, so there are greater stage drivers than their fellows and George Monroe was the greatest of all.

He was a wonder in every way. He had names for all his horses, and they all knew their names. Sometimes he spoke sharply to one or more of them, but generally he addressed them pleasantly. He seldom or never used the whip, except to crack it over their heads. Metaphorically, he spoke daggers, but used none.

He drove over my lines for nearly twenty years and never injured a person. I always put him on the box when there was a distinguished party to be driven, and fast and showy driving was expected or necessary, and he never disappointed me or exceeded the limit scheduled or fell behind.

Once he drove a party from the valley to Madera, a distance of seventy miles, in eleven hours, and in two hours afterward, in an emergency, took the reins and drove back to Wawona. Once, coming down the last grade into Mariposa, his brake broke short off while his teams were on a clean run, and he dashed the whole outfit into a chaparral clump; in less than two hours he had the animals extricated, the stage pulled out, and was trotting into Mariposa; he came into Merced on time, the fourteen passengers made up a purse of seventy dollars for him, and the two English ladies aboard sent him acceptable Christmas presents annually until I informed them of his death some years later."

Monroe, now tagged as "the greatest of all" reinsmen, verified Ulysses Grant's 1862 suggestion that African Americans, once relieved of race-based impediments, would achieve as well as any other citizen. Beyond that, Monroe had risen to the top of a demanding and exacting profession. George's family, with Grant's far-off assistance, had painstakingly overcome many of those impediments, clearing a narrow path through which George Monroe brought his talent and hard work to glorious fruition.

FIRE—*Fire at Big Tree Station.*

During winter months—the off-season for Yosemite tourism—employees of the stage company and hotel business often took alternative jobs. One frosty Saturday morning in 1878, a twenty-three-year-old stage driver named Tom Gordon was at his winter job, working alongside an expert crew of Chinese road-builders. They were near a ridge high above Big Tree Station, creating a stage road in the Mariposa Grove of Big Trees. From that point, one could see the meadow below, and on its north-west extremity on this particular morning, an ominous dark plume of rising smoke.

Gordon and the crew abandoned their equipment and rode, or ran, the six-mile, three-thousand-foot descent to join the frantic effort to save Big Tree Station. That following Saturday, readers of the *Gazette* learned the details:

"Big Tree Station Burned. — The hotel buildings of the Big Tree Station, with all their contents, were destroyed by fire on Saturday morning last. The fire originated from a defective stove pipe in the kitchen …. It is a severe blow to the Stage Company, Messrs. Washburn & Bruce, whose energy and enterprise are deserving a better fate. But it will take a fire more scorching than this one to paralyze their unyielding nerves — for the embers were not yet cool when the indomitable Washburn appeared upon the scene of the disaster, and preparations for the erection of a new building were commenced. Fortunately, there is a saw-mill upon the premises, with abundance of timber near at hand …. Mr. Joseph Shelley [*sic*], a first-class mechanic, has gone up to superintend the rebuilding. He was the architect and builder of the hotel completed at that place about two years since."[151]

Shelly's earlier hotel project for Washburn & Bruce, the 16-room so-called "Long White," now called "Clark Cottage," was saved from the fire, and at this writing is now the oldest remaining structure in the Wawona Hotel complex. Shelly's daunting new project started at a run — four weeks after the fire, the *Gazette* reported:

"Big Tree Station.—Work on the new hotel building at Big Tree Station is progressing rapidly. The planing machine which is to smooth the lumber, is ready for operation, foundations are laid. The weather has been very cold, ice forming seven inches thick—so says a young man who came down from there last Monday."[152]

Work continued through the winter, and by March 1879 the *Gazette* reported:

"The large building now in the course of construction at the Big Tree Station is said to be 140 by 32 feet and two stories high, and when completed will be the grandest hotel in the mountains of California."

The 1879 Yosemite tourist season opened at the beginning of April:

"Tourists for Yo Semite Valley.—On Tuesday last [April 1st] one of Washburn & Bruce's stages with a party of tourists, ten in number, arrived en route for the Yo Semite Valley, and stopped for [the] night at the Gallison Hotel [in Mariposa]. This is the first party to visit the Valley this season that have passed up via Mariposa ...."[153]

Arriving the next day at Big Tree Station, the ten tourists probably stayed in the sixteen-room Long White while enduring the racket of sawing and hammering from the adjacent construction site. It remains undocumented as to when the new building opened for guests, but an index of hotel registers for Big Tree Station gives the start-date for the first registry book of 1879 as June fifth. With the tourist season coming into full swing, though, it may have become necessary to make some of the rooms in the new building available

Photo-collage illustrating the relative locations of Clark's Station (left-foreground) and its two-story replacement, constructed after Clark's burned down—the two structures *never coexisted*. The two-story building still operates as the Wawona Hotel (author's collage).[154]

even while Joseph Shelly and his carpenters continued their work. At the end of June, the *Gazette* reported that Shelly was still "engaged at carpentering and milling for Washburn & Bruce at the Big Tree Station." George Monroe had recently changed his primary residence from Merced to Yosemite Valley and was likely on hand to carry the first tourists of the season along the still-muddy mountain roads.[155]

Beyond the promise of a fresh new hotel, an additional incentive for Yosemite-bound travelers was in the works. Just out of earshot from the construction site, the sound of picks, shovels, and blasting echoed through the trees a few miles to the south. In April, the *Mariposa Gazette* reported on the new project:

Mockup photo-collage showing Clark's Station circa 1876 (shown semi-transparent, on the left), where it stood relative to the current Wawona Hotel's Main Building (center). On the right is the Long White, now called Clark Cottage, which survived the fire of 1878. (Author's photographs & collage).[156]

"Thirty four Chinamen with their goods and chattels passed through this place a few days since, en route for the Big Tree Station. They are employed by Washburn & Co. to work upon the new road between the Station and Fresno Flat [now Oakhurst]."[157]

The following week's *Gazette* brought this update on the road:

"The Fresno Expositor learns from A. H. Washburn, that the new Madera and Yo Semite road will be open for travel by the first of May. A daily line of coaches will be put on at that time. The stages will leave Madera at 6 o'clock in the morning, and will reach Fresno Flats by noon, and Big Tree Station by 3 o'clock. Parties can go into the valley the same day if they desire. The return trip from the valley will be made in one day; tourists will easily save one day's time by going this route. The fare from Madera and return will be $45."[158]

Having traveled by stage for nine hours from Madera to Big Tree Station, parties opting to continue to the valley "the same day" had to endure up to five additional hours of dusty jostling, including periodic stops to change horses and take meals. Such a schedule or route that involved running stages over long distances in a single day eventually became known as the "Cannonball." This term was popularized by the flamboyant Donald R. "Cannonball" Green who founded his *Cannonball Stage Line* in 1876, which traversed vast stretches of Kansas plains in a single run. As "cannonball" refers to a schedule, rather than a particular vehicle, it is likely that any number of eight-passenger or eleven-passenger vehicles served daily as cannonball stages, depending upon the volume of ticket sales. Even after motorized Pierce-Arrow "auto-stages" replaced the horse-drawn stages in the early 20th century, Washburn's descendants referred to the through-route from Merced to Wawona as "the Cannonball."[159]

Also nearing completion was the road into the Mariposa Grove, described in these excerpts from the May 19th, 1879 issue of the *Daily Alta California*:

"One full day should also be given to the Big-tree Grove, and it would be well to have that day fixed as part of the programme of every stage-load starting for the valley—that is, after the wagon road through the grove is finished.

The road runs directly through and under the Telescope and Hamilton trees, both of which, however, must be cut out to leave room for the stages to pass.

Wahwonah Point, within the limits of the grant, has an elevation of 6540 feet, and commands an extensive view over the valley of the south fork of the Merced ....

The branch wagon-road to the Big Tree Grove is not quite finished, and will probably not be for a week to come, and tourists now go on horseback."[160]

The mention of "Wahwonah Point" is an early occurrence in print of the word thought to have meant "big tree" in local Indigenous languages, and would eventually be applied to Big Tree Station. The word had also been used earlier as a place-name by John Muir when he camped at what he called "Wawona Falls" in August 1875. An initial effort was made to carve a tunnel through the aforementioned Telescope Tree, so called because one could peer up to the sky through the fire-hollowed trunk of the living tree, but it likely became clear that the tree might not survive the mutilation. However, a second tree was indeed altered to allow the passage of stages through the base of its trunk. The article serves as a clue that it may have been the Hamilton tree that was tunneled through and then renamed the Wah-wah-nah tree. In October 1879, during Ulysses S. Grant's tour of the grove, the *San Francisco Chronicle* reported, "The coach stopped under Wah-wah-nah, and Miss Sharon took a peep up through the big telescope." In a short time, the Wawona Tree would become a world-famous icon.[161]

The Wawona Tree (Yosemite Museum and Archives)[162]

Chapter VI

GRANT — *Ulysses S. Grant and George Monroe — a detailed account.*

The pinnacle of George Monroe's career came in 1879 when Ulysses S. Grant, returning home from a two-year-long world tour, came to visit Yosemite. It would also represent a pinnacle of achievement for George's father and especially for his mother, Mary. Up to that time, Mary's and her family's travels seem to have had a synchronistic, almost numinous interconnection with Grant's, like the braided rivulets in a streambed. In the late 1840s, Mary's brother had traveled to Mexico, perhaps seeking a better life for his family, where at the same time Grant was reluctantly participating in the U.S. war of annexation that would bring slavery to the territory. In 1852, Mary's husband and brother were shadowed by Grant on their respective journeys to California, and could conceivably have even taken the same ship. Mary's route had intersected with Grant's when she journeyed through San Francisco to the gold fields in search of her husband.

These recurring coincidences punctuate a far more significant, ideological connection. Fifty-seven years had passed since the births of Mary Monroe and Ulysses S. Grant in Ohio. Both had fought for civil rights — Grant on a national level, and Mary on a very personal level, and their hard-won successes complimented one another. Grant could measure his success through stories like the Monroes,' and Mary's efforts were in part enabled by Grant. Now, carrying the weight of those difficult years, their separate but long, intertwined paths, would finally merge.

Four months before the President's visit, anticipation was already starting to grow:

"The Yo Semite travel is becoming immense. If the stage proprietors, hotel-keepers, saddle-trains, guides, etc., don't get rich, or make a good thing this season, it won't be a fault of the tourist, or effects of the new Constitution, or Grant's return from Europe."[163]

The same issue of the *Gazette* (May 31, 1879) began covering a developing story that not only would tie into Grant's visit but could also have served nicely as the basis for a certain 1962 Broadway musical — *The Music Man*. Louis Monroe, having located his "tonsorial parlor" in J. H. Miller's saloon five years earlier, had a front-row seat to the unfolding saga:

"Brass Band. — For some time past a brass band has been in embryo in this village of Mariposa, which has resulted in a partial success. The project was first gotten up and put into motion by Jos. H. Miller ...."[164]

Around the same time that Grant was traveling from China to Japan, far away on the opposite side of the Pacific a good portion of the town of Mariposa turned out to greet a freight wagon bearing a supply of sparkling new musical instruments to furnish the proposed brass band. Thomas H. DeVall, an English musician, had recently visited Mariposa with his two young sons en route to Yosemite, and Joseph Miller persuaded DeVall to become the new band director, with his musical sons as tutors. The three of them were soon performing for dances in town. The Gazette also reported that DeVall's wife accompanied them, and many months would pass before her real identity would be uncovered.[165]

Across the sea from Mariposa, in present-day Japan, Tokyo's beautiful Hama Rikyu Garden features a descriptive plaque that commemorates the site where Grant took tea with the Emperor. According to the notes in Grant's *Memoirs*:

118

"[Grant] Meets Emperor Mutsuhito (the Meiji emperor) and Empress Haruko in Tokyo, July 4; the emperor and Grant shake hands (reported to be the first time an emperor of Japan had ever done so)."[166]

Meanwhile, the young musicians of the Mariposa Brass Band, though steadily improving, were becoming restive under their temperamental leader. The *Gazette* described his "manner and mode" of teaching as "quite remarkable," but after noting that some of his pupils had become "sulky, grouty, crabbed, ill-natured, sullen and stubborn," the writer suggested that "Mr. DeVall had better change his former tactics with his pupils and treat them civilly and good-naturedly ...." Some months after Grant's Yosemite visit (and later in this narrative), disturbing news would surface regarding DeVall's relationship with his two young sons (Frederick, 13, and Herbert, 11) and the woman identified in the paper as his wife.[167]

At the beginning of September, unable to book passage for a side-trip to Australia, Grant instead headed from Japan directly to San Francisco, passing the time by reading Victor Hugo's *Les Miserables*. With the Australia trip aborted, Grant might arrive in Yosemite earlier than expected. At Big Tree Station, Joseph Shelly and his crew were likely applying the last touches to finish work, clearing away vestiges of construction debris, and readying the new hotel building and grounds for Grant's arrival. With no time to craft what would later become the hotel's signature square box columns and decorative railing, the unfinished rough-sawn four-inch posts and boards would have to suffice. Grant's ship, the "*City of Tokio*," arrived in San Francisco Saturday morning, September 20th.[168]

VIEW OF THE PARLOR AND DINING-ROOM OCCUPIED BY GENERAL GRANT AT THE PALACE HOTEL

Ulysses S. Grant in the parlor of the Palace Hotel, San Francisco, a few days before his trip to Yosemite. Behind Grant appear to be his wife, Julia, son Ulysses S. Grant Jr. (known as "Buck"), and possibly Cora Jane "Jennie" Flood, to whom Grant Jr. was engaged for a short time (illustration from *The Life of General U. S. Grant* by L. T. Remlap, 1885; author's collection).[169]

Six days before Grant's arrival at Big Tree Station, Henry Washburn hurried out from Mariposa to San Francisco, most likely to meet with Grant's party at the Palace Hotel:

"To San Francisco. —Henry Washburn, Esq., of Big Tree Station, was in town [Mariposa] Wednesday night last. He left the following day [Sep. 25] for San Francisco on business connected with the Stage Company."[170]

After crossing the bay from San Francisco, the Grant party began their two-day trek by rail and stage on September 30th. Leaving by train from Oakland at 8:30 in the morning, they reached Stockton in time for dinner at the Yosemite House, then at 7:20 p.m. continued south by rail to Madera, " ... which point they reached after midnight, and remaining in the sleeping-car during the night, started by stage directly after breakfast .... The coach which conveyed the party was handsomely decorated. Thirty-six horses were used in the trip, six changes being made."[171]

Following Washburn & Bruce's new Madera Road, Grant stopped for lunch in Fresno Flats (renamed Oakhurst in 1912). Here he was greeted with the quaint and somewhat alarming practice of anvil firing, a traditional means of celebration which involved exploding black powder between two stacked anvils, propelling the top anvil high into the air. According to the *San Francisco Chronicle*:

"At Fresno Flats, the dining place, their warmth became more earnest, they fired anvils, and, with pioneer zeal, asked the General to come and have a drink at a neighboring saloon. They pressed their request through a Committee, which threatened, in a good-natured way, to use force if he did not yield. They said: 'It's only in fun, General. Why, look a here! some of these chaps hev come twenty miles to see you.' But the General resolutely refused the saloon facilities. He ate his dinner[172] with an appetite, strolled about a little, and then, wrapping his duster about him, clambered again into his seat beside the driver. The men of Fresno Flats were Confederates during the war, and very bitter. Had he ventured over that route to Yosemite in 1865, the year the war closed, he would probably have been hanged instead of being so socially treated.

... During the last of the journey the General spoke oftener of the scenery and called Mrs. Grant's attention to it. He complimented the horses taken at the last station, praised the road and made the driver amiable by his horse-talk. The sun set when the stage was still some miles from Clark's, but the rattling pace was continued, Rapelge [*sic*, Hiram Rapelje] handling the ribbons over his six steeds as easily as by daylight. The ladies beguiled the way with songs, Mrs. Grant joining. It was 7 o'clock and very dark when a vidette stationed at some distance announced that the party was approaching. During the afternoon, a large number of people had collected."[173]

In previous weeks, Thomas DeVall and the four-month-old Mariposa Brass Band learned they had secured a performance engagement—the most prestigious imaginable. Perfecting two specific tunes from their repertoire, they would perform from the upstairs front veranda of the barely-finished hotel. Mariposa District Attorney George G. Goucher chronicled the event:

"Editor Gazette: In company with a large number from Mariposa, including the Mariposa Brass Band, we started early Wednesday morning [Oct. 1] to meet General Grant at Big Tree Station. We arrived there at about 2 P. M., and found everything in readiness for the General's reception. The hotel was tastefully decorated with evergreens, and the word 'Welcome' twined in large letters of evergreen hung conspicuously in front of the balcony. The grounds in front of the hotel were thickly planted with cedar bushes, and a splendid fountain throwing a shower of water twenty feet high added further to the attraction.

When the messenger announced the approach of the stage containing the Grant party shortly after dusk, a huge bonfire was lighted on the grounds, and the porch and balcony of the hotel illuminated with lamps, candles, etc. As the stage drove into the grounds near the hotel, the Mariposa Brass Band from the balcony struck up 'Hail to the Chief' in fine style, followed by 'Marching Thro' Georgia.' All eyes were intently fixed upon the occupants of the stage-coach as it stopped at the platform. General Grant was seated by 'Hi' [Hiram Rapelje] on the driver's seat, and his face was readily recognized from familiarity with his picture so often seen by the American people.

The party consisted of Gen. Grant, Mrs. Grant, U. S. Grant, jr., Gen. John F. Miller, wife and daughter, Miss Flood, Miss Sharon, Col. Dent and John Russell Young. Jack LaTouche, of Chowchilla Valley, who served under Grant at the 'Wilderness,' was the first to shake the General's hand, with the words, 'At the Wilderness, General,' to which Grant bowed slightly. The party was shown to rooms, and shortly after to a splendid dinner. After dinner, about 8 P.M., an informal reception was held in the sitting-room, where Grant submitted to the bore of having his hand shaken by everybody. After the ceremony some one presented the General with two cigars, and he at once showed that he appreciates such articles, and disappeared for the evening.

General Grant's well known reputation of being extremely reticent is deserved, and from our observation his travel has not changed him in that respect. His hair and beard are thickly sprinkled white, and a slight stoop in his shoulders reminds one that he is no longer young. General Grant expressed himself highly pleased by the honor paid by the Mariposa Brass Band in receiving him at the Station." [174]

Goucher's account of the ten passengers indicates that the party rode in on an eleven-passenger stage, rather than a smaller eight-passenger stage. These larger stages featured three upholstered bench-seats, plus room for two passengers next to the driver. A *San Francisco Chronicle* correspondent described the scene outside Big Tree Station:

"All the population of Mariposa had come out, including its aristocracy, its District Attorney, and a brass band, composed chiefly of smooth faced boys, who had just begun musical practice. The smaller towns had sent representatives; the ranchers in the distant canyons had left their crops ungarnered and rode on horseback over the high ridges. Among the rest, were soldiers who had served with Grant; there were a few who had served against him.

A small delegation of [Indigenous people] helped to swell the gathering, which was motley in apparel but uniform in admiration. Besides these there were some English tourists, deeply interested, though the matter was so foreign to their sympathies. The hotel, which is the two-story building replacing the one destroyed by fire last fall, was tastefully decorated.

… As the stage dashed round to the steps of the portico the band played 'Hail to the Chief,' and there was a rush from all parts of the house to the front. The stage never brought a dustier company to Yosemite; they were covered with it as with an extra garment. The General looked as if he had been engaged a week in the most hotly contested Battle of the Wilderness."[175]

The road dust, sometimes referred to as "pulverized scenery," was typically brushed from the clothes of arriving guests by hotel personnel wielding feather-dusters.

As reported by District Attorney Goucher, the first man to greet the President was Jack LaTouche, a much-admired local farmer-homesteader and family man, who had indeed served with the 19th Massachusetts Infantry under Grant at the Battle of the Wilderness.[176]

Big Tree Station Main Building, still under construction, c. 1879 (Mariposa Museum and History Center Collection)[177]

The *San Francisco Chronicle* correspondent wrote a less flattering description of LaTouche before going on to describe the evening's events:

"The first to shake hands with him was a veteran inebriate, who claimed to have fought under his banner in the siege of Vicksburg. He was spared further hand-shaking at the moment, and half an hour later the entire party—General Grant with Mrs. Miller, and General Miller with Mrs. Grant—

125

entered the dining room and took their places at the table. General Grant occupied one end and John Russell Young the other. The dining room was neatly decorated with evergreens. The menu, which had been prepared with special care, included little beside the products of the region — peaches, pears and melons from the valley near the station, and deer, grouse, mountain and lowland quail, and mountain trout from the region around aiding to furnish as excellent entertainment.

As the hour was late, most of the guests had left the room before the General's party made their appearance. While conversing with Mr. Washburn during dinner, General Grant was asked if he had ever been in Yosemite. He said he had not; in 1851 [*sic*, possibly 1852 and/or 1854], before the valley was known, except to a few pioneers, he came to Tuolumne in the employ of the Government. At the village and in riding about the region he spent fourteen days.

… He complimented everything about him — the hotels, the table and the band, evidently not expecting so much attention in so wild a locality. After dinner some of the young ladies, being indisposed, retired at once to their rooms. The rest, with Mrs. Grant and Mrs. Miller, took chairs in the public sitting room. The General mingled a while with the crowd, then took a place near one of the doors and went through the usual process of hand-shaking, the mountaineers being introduced by A. H. Washburn.

The scene, with its homely surroundings, Mrs. Grant and the ladies of her party sitting by in rocking chairs while the General shook hands with the mountain yeomanry, was one of extremely rural simplicity. The reception was over in half an hour, and then the General with his party retired to their rooms. That assigned to the General and Mrs. Grant was a plain but very comfortable bed-chamber, furnished in walnut hung with Yosemite views and having an outlook to the west to the Devil's Nose, crowned with its plume-like pines."[178]

Henry Washburn's wife, Jean Bruce Washburn, wrote to her brother Albert about the evening. Her letter alludes to some unpleasantness, but key sections of the letter appear to have been physically redacted:

"Met the President & wife with party; was charmed with the President & wife—put on no airs but talked with me as pleasantly as if my friends, on governmental affairs and their [opinions], are the sweetest most unassuming couple I ever met to be so high in position, their [satellites] were more airy, Miss Sherman [probably Miss Flora Sharon] is plain and simple in manner and good looking. Mrs. Presidentess is a rosy robust good natured cheery person, with dark grey blue eyes, black hair, and full round good featured face.

An English Member of Parliament said she was perfectly delicious (curious expression). [Rest of the paragraph indecipherable; corner of the page is torn off]. We were delightfully at home together yet I could not induce the folks to cheer them or [page torn off] him [his?] … [tear the horn] off an anvil. I decorated the parlor [3 words torn off] one shifted it & all my ferns [5 words torn off]. Some spite!! to them politics I suppose. They came and left without the slightest recognition of their position."[179]

Mrs. Washburn's fragmented letter invokes an old saying about one who could "tear the horn off an anvil," referring to somebody prone to breaking things. It would appear that some unruly visitors had not only moved (or knocked over?) some of her interior decorations but had failed to show respect for the honored guests due to political differences.

Meanwhile, George Monroe was most likely drifting off to sleep in the men's bunkhouse, lulled by the nearby river sounds, and reviewing in his mind every detail of the next day's duties, for he would be the president's stage-driver.

Early in the morning, after pulling on his best driving clothes and downing a good breakfast, Monroe would put the last touches on the stage, checking the hardware, hitching the horses, giving a last wipe-down of the leather bench-seats, and counting the stack of folded cotton dusters available for passengers to protect their fine clothing from the road dust. After donning his own fresh duster, Monroe would drive uphill from the stage-barn to the hotel, where a crowd was already gathering.

With the doors of the new hotel building on his left, Monroe guided his team to within inches of the stage platform, allowing level access to the stage for his passengers. Monroe sat on the right-front seat of the stage with his right foot on the brake, calming the horses and greeting his passengers while the band played and the crowd pressed toward the platform.

District Attorney Goucher was again on hand to chronicle the occasion, documenting a rare bit of quoted dialogue from Monroe:

"At 8:00 a.m. Thursday morning the Grant party started for Yo Semite, accompanied by the Mariposa Brass Band. As Mrs. Grant mounted the seat of the coach, she showed some anxiety by asking Geo. Monroe, the driver, 'Are you a good driver?' to which he modestly replied, 'No, Ma'am.'"[180]

General Grant climbed in and took his place on the front bench seat, directly to Monroe's left. Monroe eased his foot off the brake, and with a motion of his reins and a gentle vocal nudge to the team of six horses, the crowd parted and the stage began to move, following the circle drive in a gradual arc slowly to the right. Halfway around the circle, with the hotel (and the band) now well off to their right, Monroe swung his team of horses in a slight left turn and down a short steep hill, his right foot riding the brake, rolling northward toward the covered bridge.

Though unreported, it is probable that Louis and Mary Monroe were on hand. Knowing their son would be carrying Grant that Thursday morning, and given Mary's steely determination, nothing was likely to deter them from this once-in-a-lifetime chance to witness their son's place in history.

More than a century later, Yosemite National Park still offered stage rides through that very same bridge, with modern passengers experiencing the same sights, smells, and sounds as Grant had that morning with the bridge vibrating from the booming of hooves and rattle of the stage. Aboard a re-creation of a Washburn stage, emerging from the covered bridge and thinking back to that cool October morning, one could envision an intense but fleeting glance, suspended in time as in an antique photograph, as George's eyes caught those of his parents.

Perhaps Grant saw them, too, positioned as he was in the place of honor next to George Monroe. Seated behind were Grant's wife and son bouncing in tandem with the stage, counterpointed by the jostling crowd, all breathing the dust kicked up by the horses, all caught up in the moment, sharing the experience.

Children of the same time and place, their widely divergent paths nonetheless connected, the lives of Ulysses Grant and Mary Monroe had finally converged. Relying upon the skill of George Monroe, the president rode next to Mary's son: two Americans with extraordinary backgrounds, seated on a level bench. Eighteen years later, Mary's brother could have been speaking for George Monroe as well as for himself, when he declared before a jury, "I claim to be an American, sir—I do not claim it, it is simply a fact … if we stood on a level we would be just on a level."

Photograph believed to be of a Yosemite stage station; the man on the left is wearing what appears to be a leather blacksmith's apron (Courtesy Patty Malone)[181]

Changing horses at Chinquapin Barn, halfway between Wawona and Yosemite Valley (Yosemite Museum and Archives)

The stage would have stopped to change horses periodically. There was Eight Mile Station and Eleven Mile Station, so called because of their distances from the Covered Bridge, and about halfway between Big Tree Station and Yosemite Valley was Chinquapin Station. Chinquapin marked the highest elevation of that day's trip—5,866 feet above sea level. Stopping at the stage company barn while a crew deftly swapped the six horses for a fresh team, Grant and his family would have a short break to stand and stretch, visit the outhouse, or take a drink of water and admire the forest scenery. Continuing downhill toward Grouse Creek Station, the travelers would have been treated to the first of the year's fall colors, dogwoods with bright reds, black-oak trees dressed in a stately bronze, and big-leaf maples flashing bright yellow, described a few months later by Galen Clark:

"We have had one of the finest Autumns that I have ever seen here .... Never before have I seen Yosemite so brilliant with the rich and gorgeous colors and tints of Autumn. All the deciduous leaves seemed to assume their bright and most fascinating holiday colors ...."[182]

Though much of the stage road is now occupied by the current Wawona Road, there are a few places where the two roads diverge, most significantly where the stage road drops downhill to the west to what is still called Elevenmile Meadow, and further along at Grouse Creek. At Grouse Creek Station, Monroe may have offered to stop at the stage-barn or even changed horses there, though the downhill travel would not have taxed the horses as much as the grade from Wawona up to Chinquapin. At Grouse Creek, the stage road once again departs from the current road, staying uphill while the newer Wawona Road heads down to the nearly mile-long Wawona Tunnel—an expensive bit of 1930s engineering not likely to have been contemplated by Washburn's road-builders in 1875.

Monroe's stage would encounter another stage-station near the Hermitage (mentioned earlier), a location that one day would bear George Monroe's name. Each of the stage-stations typically had horse-barns, employee accommodations, a water source, a corral and feed for the horses, and provisions for the stages. Shortly beyond the Hermitage was Inspiration Point, where Monroe would pull the horses to a stop, set the break on the stage, help his passengers to the ground, and for the hundredth time listen to the familiar gasps and exclamations as his passengers spent a little time with the incomparable view. Modern visitors parking their cars at the "Tunnel View" on the Wawona Road can walk up the switchback trail to the old stage road and Inspiration Point, and stand where George Monroe stood as he soothed his team of horses and answered his passengers' questions.

The thrill of Inspiration Point was compounded by the next stretch of road, a steep downhill grade headed straight toward the base of Bridal Veil Fall, leveling out upon reaching the valley floor.

Now within the granite walls, amid a canopy of colorful leaves and the nutty fragrance of autumn in Yosemite Valley, Monroe could allow the horses to assume a more leisurely pace. Rolling beneath the shadow of Sentinel Rock, Monroe would have pointed out the newly dedicated Yosemite Chapel as they passed by. Only six years later Monroe would drive the stage carrying famed composer Sir Arthur Sullivan to that same chapel, where Sullivan would play the organ for Grant's memorial service.[183]

Monroe evidently won over Mrs. Grant during the trip, as Monroe was heard to remark to a bystander, "I never hauled a lady over these roads who was so enthusiastic." In his dual occupation as driver and tour guide, Monroe answered Grant's questions about distances and the heights of various cliffs and waterfalls.[184] Though unreported, the president's stage was surely followed by other stages carrying local dignitaries, reporters, and the like. Along the road would have been knots of onlookers who had come to Yosemite to get a glimpse of Grant. As he entered Yosemite Valley, the rattle of the stage and the muted sound of twenty-four hooves drumming the soft, dusty road would be punctuated by echoes of black powder explosions. This peculiar greeting concocted by locals to impress the president, and reminiscent of the "anvil-firing" that took place during his visit to Fresno Flats, serves to illustrate the level of training and control that Monroe and his fellow drivers had perfected to keep their horses calm amid teeming crowds and sharp noises.

The intrepid Mariposa Brass Band must have left Big Tree Station very early in the morning—early enough to be on hand to welcome the president and his party at Barnard's Hotel in Yosemite Valley with, once again, "Hail to the Chief."[185]

In his 1903 article, Ben C. Truman recalled the trip in his typically colorful prose:

"In all the galleries of Sierra Knights, from Shasta to Tehachapi, George Monroe ... was the monarch of all; and when General Grant visited the Yosemite Valley nearly a quarter of a century ago, he was accompanied, from Merced to Wawona by Henry Washburn (lately deceased), one of the proprietors of the Yosemite Stage and Turnpike Company; and from that point to the Valley, the General and his party were driven by Monroe, then about twenty-six [sic, thirty-two], and conceded to be the best man that ever held the reins over six horses along that extremely beautiful twenty-six miles of road.[186]

As is well known by all visitors to the Yosemite, by Wawona, this stretch is a continuous succession of the letter S, winding in and out in many places so sharply as to make the turns seem nearly impossible or thrillingly dangerous and to make the three teams of horses form the three sides of the letter.[187]

The General sat with the driver, of course, and was in ecstasies all the way, as he had never witnessed such a splendid exhibition of mountain driving before. George Monroe was also in a paroxysm of joy .... As he sat there, with his six lines and long whip, with one foot on the brake and the other braced against the footboard, he arrested the attention of the illustrious American soldier and traveler by his side, for he appeared to have as perfect control of Henry Washburn's selected horses as if the whole turnout were an automaton. He would throw those six animals from one side to the other to avoid a stone or a chuckhole as if they were a machine or a single quadruped; sometimes a hub would just gently scrape the bank on the upper side, and in a moment afterward infinitesimally overlap the precipice on the down side.

Crack! went his whip, every once in a while, and down would go the teams on a rapturous canter, and around the sharp curves and over plank culverts, and up again on a clean run the crack of the whips making piccolo screeches amidst the thunders of the coach and the rushing waters. Had the reins been electric ribbons or delicate galvanic threads, or tissues of life, they could not have more adequately or omnipotently conveyed the thoughts and designs of the handsome Jehu to the equine sextette, whose dilating nostrils and palpitating bodies told of a movement that had probably never been equaled since the daring son of Nimshi drove furiously six thousand years ago.[188]

John Russell Young once referred to General Grant as the Sphinx. But there was another beside him that day, for Monroe never spoke a word nor turned his head. The two were a 'Sitting Colossi' in flesh and blood. After the stop at Inspiration Point, however, they mutually relaxed and indulged in conversation until the Valley was reached, when Monroe handed the lines and the whip to the General, but maintained his seat and foot at the brake. In a few years afterward, Monroe took President and Mrs. [Rutherford B.] Hayes over the same route, and treated them to some of his most artistic driving."

Such purple prose must have helped to elevate Monroe's status. Years later, stories of Monroe would wend their way into the fabric of Yosemite legend, as in this reminiscence from 1926:

"Tales are told of the rollicking speed at which these stagecoaches sometimes traveled over the then perilous roads. The Black Devil's Turn was a particularly perilous bend, so named for the negro driver who generally managed to take it on two wheels, giving his passengers an unbilled extra thrill."[189]

Illustration by Pierre N. Boeringer, misattributed as that of George Monroe [190]

In a romanticized nostalgia piece from 1924, Truman's description of George Monroe was quoted in the *Oakland Tribune*, omitting any reference to his racial heritage, and misattributing an image as being that of Monroe.

Truman wrote that Monroe "had never permitted but one man to take the reins from him in his life, and that was President Grant." Though Truman's 1903 article had Monroe driving Grant from Wawona to Yosemite Valley, his 1898 article told a different story, purporting to quote Monroe:

"The General drove nearly all the way to Inspiration Point," said [Monroe], "and lighted at least four cigars. He took in everything along the road and made all the turns as perfectly as an old driver. I had a fine crowd that day, — the General and Mrs. Grant and Ulysses, Jr.; Mr. [John Russel] Young, who has since been Minister to China and — is now Librarian of Congress; and there was Miss Jennie Flood, the only daughter of the wealthy bonanza man, who was jilted by young ['Buck'] Grant; Miss Dora Miller, the only daughter of Senator [John F.] Miller, who is now the wife of Commander [Richardson] Clover, United States Navy, and Miss Flora Sharon, who afterwards married Sir Thomas Hesketh of England.

Miss Sharon was the prettiest girl I ever carried into the valley, and Mrs. Langtry the most beautiful and agreeable woman. I have received presents from all the members of the Grant family. The General himself gave me a silver-mounted cigar-case containing eight cigars, and the girls sent me gloves and candy."

How much of the preceding was actually spoken by Monroe, and how Lillie Langtry got wedged into the narrative (her visit wasn't until 1884), perhaps doesn't matter as much as the color provided by Truman.

Two other drivers in Washburn's employ carried the presidential party: Hiram "Hi" Rapelje had brought Grant from Madera to Big Tree Station via Washburn's newly opened Madera Road, and Wesley Barton "Billy" Dowst would pilot the six-horse eleven-passenger stage from Big Tree Station to Merced via Mariposa:

"'Captain' Dowst, the most ancient driver of California, is an elephant when it devolves upon him to give velocity to a four-wheeled [stage] drawn by six horses. Gen Grant ought to remember Dowst, Hi Rapelgee [sic] and George Monroe …." [191]

Fred Schlageter in June 1915, holding Wawona Washburn (Hartwig) in front of what is now called "Moore Cottage" at the Wawona Hotel. (Yosemite Museum & Archives)

Fred Schlageter was the second-chair B-flat cornetist in the Mariposa Brass Band, and on that first day of October 1879 was celebrating his 20th birthday as he played "Hail to the Chief" for the president. Fred's father, Herman, ran the hotel where Louis Monroe had once worked as a barber. In 1941, Fred Schlageter left this reminiscence:

"'General Grant arrived by way of the Chowchilla Road by stagecoach, and spent the night at Wawona. He came into

138

the valley on October 1. While in the valley he stayed at the Yosemite Falls Hotel (Old Sentinel), which was considered the best place to stop at that time. There had been much talk of General Grant's visit into the valley, and the place was full of campers who had come in from as far as Stockton days before. The day the General arrived the people were lined up everywhere to see him; three sticks of dynamite were shot off and the band lined up in front of the hotel and played 'Hail to the Chief' and several other numbers. The General then shook hands with the band players. He hired a horse from George Monroe (a negro stage driver) and rode around the valley. Mr. Schlageter stated that at Mirror Lake the band players rowed around the lake in row boats and that there was dancing on the platform there; also fishing in Mirror Lake.

On October 3 [*sic* October 5], the General's party left the valley, stayed overnight at Wawona, and visited the Mariposa Grove. A stage driver by the name of Dave Douse [*sic*, Wesley Dowst] drove the General from Wawona to Mariposa where the party had lunch and then went on to Merced.'

Jack Leidig, who was with Mr. Schlageter at the time he gave the above record, added that at the time of General Grant's visit to the park, he was 5 ½ years old. The day the General arrived small Jack was out riding with his father dressed in his best 'bib and tucker.' His father got out of the buggy to shake hands with the General and Jack decided that the General and Henry Washburn looked enough alike to be brothers."[192]

John Russell Young, one of Grant's party, recalled, "A few days were spent in the Yosemite, every point of interest in the valley being visited. The General climbed the rocks, rode over the peaks, and seemed to enjoy once more the freedom and the motion of out-door life."[193]

"Cannon Ball Stage—Mr. Fobes—with Ray" (c. 1880) Yosemite Stage & Turnpike Co. stage driver Charles Fobes poses with his son, Ray, in Yosemite Valley (Yosemite Museum and Archives)

Galen Clark recalled:

"Among the visitors to the Yosemite, the past season, there has been quite a number of European Nobility, Earls, Barons, Lords, Sir Knights and Military Officials. But none more distinguished and world renowned than our own fellow citizen Gen. U. S. Grant. His visit and reception here was very quiet, and without much parade or show, though every one strove to have the honor of taking him by the hand and rendering him such services as were in their power. Giant powder was used for firing salutes, and awakening up the echoes and reverberations around the valley. Barnard's Hotel, where the General and party stopped, and several other buildings, were adorned with evergreens and banners; and the word 'Welcome' was often seen as well as heard. The General seemed to enjoy his visit here very much. He said that the valley came quite up to his expectations, and that he should have to come again when not so pressed for time."[194]

The following account covers the return, Sunday, October 5, from Yosemite Valley to Big Tree Station and a tour of the Mariposa Grove. It includes another instance of Grant taking the reins for part of the trip, and a rare anecdote involving Grant and Monroe:

"AT THE BIG TREES.
Return of the Grant Party from Yosemite Valley.
[Special Dispatch to the Chronicle.]

Merced, October 6.— … the General is now returning to San Francisco fatigued but gratified. He left Yosemite with his party on Sunday morning …. The stage left Bernard's Hotel, in Yosemite Valley, at 7 a.m., George Monroe holding the ribbons, and the General and Mrs. Grant on the box. He has sat with the driver on every stage coach since he left the railroad, and led on every trail—he has made it a matter of pride always to be at the head of the column. The inside of the stage was packed closely, the young ladies and Ulysses, Jr., preferring the front seats. As the stage sped down the

141

valley, it stopped to bid good-by to friends at Black's Hotel. The morning was as quiet as the early Sabbath in so remote a place could well be. The east wall of the valley was still in shadow, which extended to the foot of El Capitan and Eagle Peak ....

There were only two stoppages on the way—one for a ten-minute picnic, and the other caused by the breaking of a bolt, which was soon repaired. This slight accident was the only one on the trip, there having before this been only little annoyances from yellow-jackets on the trails. The occurrence entailed a change of General and Mrs. Grant to a buggy, developing in the General some of the old horse instinct, he taking the reins and driving neatly into the station over the few miles of mountain road that remained. The flags were floating on the hotel, and its front still bore all the blazonry of welcome. After lunch, the party drove up the new road to

THE BIG TREES

Starting about 2 o'clock. There they went through the usual routine. The General was impressed by the massive proportions of the Grizzly Giant. The coach stopped under Wah-wah-nah, and Miss Sharon took a peep up through the big telescope. [Author's note: at the time, many of the giant sequoia trees were emblazoned with plaques bearing the names of persons and places, or descriptive titles]. At the little cabin called Galen's Hospice all the party alighted, and both ladies and gentlemen walked about on the prostrate form of Andy Johnson. This tree fell only a week before Johnson's death. The Giants, General Grant, Ohio, Illinois and Ike Cook were all very closely inspected. While looking at the first the guide told the General a story of Judge Jackson of Georgia, who with a friend was visiting the grove, and who were about taking their lunch in the shadow of the tree which bears the name of the great Union General. He called their attention to the fact and they at once moved over and finished their repast near a more congenial spirit—Andrew Johnson. The General heard the story, smiled one of his slow, wise smiles, and said nothing."[195]

Only thirteen years before, President Andrew Johnson had opposed equal rights for African Americans. Judge Henry Rootes Jackson had served as a major general in the Confederate States Army during the Civil War. Monroe's confidence in telling this rather loaded story to Grant, combined with the earlier story of Monroe's "No, Ma'am" response to Mrs. Grant's nervous question, gives a tantalizing suggestion of Monroe's possessing a wry sense of nuance. It is easy to imagine why he was popular with the Yosemite tourist elite, and in this case was able to elicit Grant's slow, wise smile in that quiet and deeply significant moment of camaraderie.

Grant's ever-present biographer, John Russell Young, recalled, " … we spent an hour or two wandering about, clambering over fallen trunks, and endeavoring to form some idea of the real magnitude of these gigantic phenomena of nature …."[196]

Monday morning, the sixth of October, Grant departed Big Tree Station for San Francisco. Instead of returning via the newly-opened Madera Road, Washburn purposely directed the stage to bring the President along the well-worn Mariposa route. The *Gazette* observed,

"Mr. Henry Washburn deserves the thanks of our entire community for bringing Gen. Grant over this route, and we believe some of our people were nearly as glad to see Henry's genial face as they were any of the Grant Party."[197]

Upon his arrival in Mariposa, Grant was greeted by the usual crowds and practically all of the local African American population including, notably, Union Army veteran Alexander Pelton:

"When former President Grant stopped [in Mariposa] …, in addition to receiving a rousing welcome from many of the white citizens, the negroes, every one of them, went to the hotel and shook hands, with their great friend. One of the negroes, who seemed especially delighted to see the former President, was Aleck Pelton, and from the mutual greeting, it was evident that the two had met previously."[198]

According to his military pension card, Pelton had served in the volunteer 3rd Regiment Iowa Cavalry, Company L, and was now living with his wife and grandchild in Hornitos, working in the mines and hiring out as a laborer for local ranchers.[199]

Again, the indomitable Mariposa Brass Band had scrambled ahead to serenade Grant's arrival in Mariposa, with encore performances of "Hail to the Chief" and "Marching Through Georgia," though by this time Theodore Smith of Hornitos had replaced Thomas DeVall as leader of the band.[200]

Perhaps explaining why the young bandmembers had earlier been reported as being "sulky, grouty, crabbed, ill-natured, sullen and stubborn," a *Gazette* article in 1880 reported an unfortunate coda to DeVall's story. While acknowledging DeVall's success in organizing the band, it was observed that he was "extremely irritable and impatient," given to "unbecoming language" and becoming "threatening and abusive." After leaving Mariposa he took up residence in Stockton, California, where he was soon arrested and fined $100 for "cruelty to children," having exploited his two sons as "musicians in a public place and for money." Soon after it was learned that the woman traveling with DeVall was not his wife, and though his sons were being compelled to call her "mamma," they "desired to go to their mother … but were prevented by their father." According to the report, "DeVall and the woman were trying to leave the state" when they were apprehended, and the sons were reunited with their real mother in San Francisco.[201]

Having finished construction of the "grandest hotel in the mountains of California," Joseph Shelly moved with his family to Bishop Creek (now Bishop, California) by July 1880. His three creations, the Main Building, the Long White (now Clark Cottage), and per Shelly family tradition, the Covered Bridge, endure to this day as part of the Wawona Hotel complex.[202]

George Monroe had now become a watched celebrity in the local papers with blurbs like this one in March 1881:

"J. K. Barnard and wife, of Yo Semite, and George T. Monroe [sic], a celebrated reinsman, of Washburn & Bruce, were stopping at the Palace Hotel in San Francisco, on the 21st instant."[203]

At the time, Monroe's employers had business ties with the prestigious Palace Hotel, having installed a travel agent at that location.[204] In August 1881 the *Gazette* reported on another item in connection with Monroe and the Palace Hotel:

"Handsome Fawns. —We noticed a pair of the handsomest fawns we ever laid our eyes on last Friday morning. They were caught by a sheep-herder near Big Tree Station, purchased by George Monroe, and sent by him as a gift, to the Palace Hotel, San Francisco."[205]

The fate of the fawns remains unreported.

145

Chapter VII

TRIUMPH—*George Monroe's fame as a stage-driver, his parents lauded by the press, and Washburn dominates Yosemite tourism.*

The Monroe family was experiencing what must have seemed a *belle époque*—a beautiful age—especially when they looked back upon their difficult past. George Monroe, now in his thirties, had distinguished himself as an expert teamster and achieved wide acclaim. His parents had established a secure income through their ranch in the pastoral Sierra foothills. George, too, was secure in his job and had joined the fortunate few who could call Yosemite Valley their home.

It is not surprising that George seems to have kept his youthful exuberance. Much of his time off the job was spent exercising his horse, a sorrel mare that he called Lady Lightfoot. Though his work hours were usually spent piloting stages at a measured pace amid clouds of dust, on his days off he and Lady Lightfoot could cut loose, roam the trails and roads, and feel the fresh, scented air in one of the most beautiful places on earth. At times, Monroe might be seen urging his mare into a full-out gallop, dashing along the meadows of Yosemite Valley.

Ed Washburn and his brother, John, had returned to California in 1878 to join Henry in running the hotel business along with John Bruce. Interestingly, by 1881 Bruce's uncle, Albert O. Bruce, was working for Moses Rodgers at the Washington Mine in Hornitos. Rodgers also had become a co-owner of the Eureka Mine that Washburn and John Bruce had leased back in 1865.[206]

Sixteen years had passed since Washburn left the mining business to pursue Yosemite tourism, and sixteen years since Rodgers was elected, under Louis Monroe's chairmanship, to represent the Mariposa area at the 1865 "Colored Convention." Much of the promise and optimism of that convention had come to pass—Moses Rodgers was now a highly successful mine engineer and owner, and Louis and Mary Monroe now owned and operated a large ranch. George Monroe had become the most famous employee of Washburn and Bruce, whose Yosemite Stage & Turnpike Company now boasted an inventory of 173 horses, with 27 vehicles in their "rolling stock" that included nineteen stages.[207]

In August 1881, a writer for the *Mariposa Gazette* described a personal tour of the Mariposa Grove that was led by John Bruce:

" ... The idea of a large stage-coach loaded with passengers, drawn by six horses, passing through one of the monster trees at its base or trunk, sounds like a fairy tale, but it's a fact, nevertheless.

... We were accompanied to the big trees by Mr. and Mrs. Bruce and their children, who, with our own force, made up a complement of thirteen, who took passage in a four-horse stage with Mr. Fred Brightman as reinsman.

... On our return Mr. Bruce directed the stage to the Fish Camp, a place of some note on the Madera road ...."[208]

Just seven months after the excursion, in March 1882, Johnny Bruce died unexpectedly at age 45, reportedly from a seizure.[209]

Though mourning the loss of his nephew and longtime partner, Henry and his two brothers soldiered ahead, continuing to invest and grow their business. At the same time, Mary and Louis Monroe were expanding and improving the family farm near Mariposa. In the 1880 census, Louis now gave his occupation as farmer and seems to have closed his tonsorial saloon around this time, and George, having moved to Yosemite Valley, is no longer listed as one of the household. Louis Monroe added acreage to Mary's original land claim with new pre-emptions in 1880 and 1884, as did George in 1881, 1883, and early 1886, bringing their combined holdings to an impressive 480 acres.[210] Mary's brother, George Millen, rejoined the family after twenty years of blacksmithing in Trinity County, setting up shop on the Monroe property by 1884.[211]

Monroe Ranch site (Author photograph)

The countryside encompassing the Monroes' ranch was described in the *Gazette* with prose and poetry, giving the impression that Louis and Mary lived in a place of rural contentment:

"FROM PEA RIDGE.
Pea Ridge, Mariposa Co., April 15th, 1881

Editor Gazette:

This place is called Pea Ridge because no peas grow here, nor do I believe they ever will until a new dispensation is ordered. Peas are not a specialty here; besides, the place is not a ridge at all, but many round hills divided by small valleys and innumerable water courses. The soil is a sandy loam, very good for grain and hay, which the people raise in small quantities. The geographical boundaries of Pea Ridge are not well defined, but it appears to be several miles wide by a few more in length ....

There is no better grain land in the State than this, and a crop is sure if sown early. Fruit is not much cultivated, but where it is grown shows a fair average. The pasturage is excellent, and attracts many stockraisers in spring ....

You all, no doubt, have heard or known
Of that beautiful place of sand and stone,
Pea Ridge they call it, or let it alone;
And some have rented and some do own
Its acres, scooped like a barley 'scone;'
Where the women are pretty, the men are tall,
And all the males, both great and small,
Are patched on the butt like a rifle-ball.[212]

The children are many, and there they stay
From the hour of birth till their heads are gray —
'Twould be their ruin if they should stray
Out into the light of the living day;
Besides, it is hard to get away
From the poison oak and chapparal
And the hot, fierce sun that warms up all
The strong emotions in 'boy and gal,'
To a heat that would colder souls appall.

150

In the 'balmy spring, when the calves are fat
And ready for the rope and lariat,
The honest Pea Ridger begins to feel
A love of grain slightly mixed with steel;
And tying a long spur on his heel,
Makes the cattle 'blate' and the porkers squeal.

At the close of the day his heart is big,
As he eats the flesh of the juicy pig;
And the happy children around him laugh
While securing their neighbor's 'fatted calf.'"[213]

It wasn't all bucolic splendor at Pea Ridge, though, after gold was discovered less than two miles from the Monroe ranch:

"Silver Ore.—Captain Cady, of the Hambleton Silver Mining Company, was in town one day this week, and brought with him some fine specimens of silver ore. The rock shows the pure metal, and it needs neither glasses to see nor smelting to prove it. Notwithstanding the silver is visible all through the rock, yet it is claimed that gold predominates by a large percentage. We shall yet, we hope, soon be able to announce rich developments from this section. Two companies are at work, machinery is being provided for, and everything looks propitious for a valuable mining interest."[214]

By 1883, the mine, featuring a 250' shaft, was estimated to produce up to $100 per ton—a yield that would attract unwanted clamor, punctuating the Monroes' otherwise peaceful surroundings with the sound of blasting and the hammering of a stamp mill.

Up in Yosemite Valley, we find George and Lady Lightfoot enjoying a day at the races:

"Items from Yosemite Valley.

Yosemite Valley, Sept. 6, 1881.

Editor of the Gazette:

The races that were announced for last Saturday were postponed and came off on Monday, the 5th instant.

First race, for citizens' purse, $30, 2 half-mile heats; $5 entrance; three or more to start; second horse, save entrance money—Three entries, viz: Capt. Samuel Tilden enters bay horse 'Johnnie-from-town;' George Monroe enters sorrel mare 'Lady Lightfoot;' Col. A. H. Harris enters gray horse 'Limber Jim.' First heat won by 'Johnnie-from-town;' second horse, 'Limber Jim;' third, 'Lady Lightfoot.' Second heat same as the first, except 'Lady Lightfoot' beating 'Limber Jim.' Purse and race awarded to 'Johnnie-from-town.' Time, 54 seconds.

Second race—John Wesley Woods' roan colt 'Nick-of-the-Woods,' and G. Monroe's 'Lady Lightfoot.' 'Lady Lightfoot' leaves the track and 'Nick-of-the-Woods' gets away with the cash ....

Racing kept up until dark, and well attended by ladies and gents. Everything passed off pleasantly, with much fun and a good time generally."[215]

In 1882 the Monroes' industriousness—and particularly that of Mary Monroe—brought well-deserved accolades in the local press:

"A Visit to Monroe's Ranch.—On Sunday last, we with our partner and baby, visited the home and ranch of Mr. and Mrs. L. A. Monroe, about six miles southeast of Mariposa. Here we were pleased to find a couple, who through frugal industry have built up for themselves one of the pleasantest and most thrifty homes to be found in the foothills of the Sierras adjacent to Mariposa.

They have two quarter sections of land which they have acquired by homestead and pre-emption a large portion of which is arable, and productive of cereals of all kinds, of the best average per acre. Their farm, and the country around, abounds with lasting springs of water, ample for stock and gardening purposes, during the driest seasons that have so far occurred.

Mrs. Monroe is a most remarkable woman for her individual energy and extraordinary skill in her management of affairs usually belonging to the opposite sex. She executes the work of a carpenter building gates, barns, sheds, out buildings, fences, hay frames and many other conveniences necessary to a home and farm. The indications of thrift and industry are manifest at every point about the premises. A complete outfit of farming utensils, consisting of a reaper, thresher, cultivator, a new wagon and other implements necessary for farming, fill the sheds. Besides, there are horses, cows, stock cattle, hogs and chickens sufficient to assure a good annual income, and ample to live upon.

We took dinner with our friends, who extended to us a kindly welcome which we shall not soon forget. After taking a limited survey of the surroundings, we bade them adieu for the present."[216]

George continued to draw recognition, too, in this case through a travel journal published in 1884:

"Our driver was a colored man, raised in the country, had never been outside of the State and had been with the Yosemite Stage Co. some twelve years. His gentleness and kindness were only exceeded by his skill, of which we soon became both proud and grateful."[217]

153

The same year, the familiar destination on George's itinerary, Big Tree Station (formerly Clark & Moore's), was now (reluctantly by some) being called Wawona:

"The name of Big Tree Station has been changed to Wawona, Indian name for 'big tree.' Ed Washburn, the popular agent of Wawona, has returned to Merced for the winter. John Washburn of Wawona was registered at El Capitan Hotel yesterday. (Too much 'Wawona'—it won't stick. —Editor, Gazette.)"[218]

Much of the public and press, perhaps irate over the name change, would staunchly continue to call the place "Big Tree Station," and many others stuck to its older, venerable appellation of "Clark's."

Ca. 1915—Fully loaded eleven-passenger stage in front of the Wawona Hotel, John Washburn standing on right, with (possibly) his son, Clarence Washburn, driving the stage. (Author's collection)

Over the past fifteen years, the Monroes had acquired their land, piece by piece, through pre-emption under the Homestead Act of 1862. Having received United States citizenship through the Civil Rights Act of 1866, African Americans over the age of 21 could legally claim up to a quarter-section (160 acres) of public land (land owned by the federal government). It wasn't free; after 6 months of residency on the property, claimants wanting to own the land had to come up with $1.25 per acre, as well as yearly property taxes. By 1886, each of the Monroes had both claimed and purchased their individual maximums of 160 acres from the government.[219]

All of this likely required legal assistance, and in those pre-telephone days, the only way for Louis and Mary to ascertain whether their lawyer was in his office was to make the six-mile buggy ride into Mariposa:

"Mr. and Mrs. L. A. Monroe were in town on Wednesday. They had legal business to be attended to, but their attorney had gone to the country, which will necessitate their coming again."[220]

Two weeks later, on May 30, 1885, this ad appeared in the *Gazette*:

"NEW TO-DAY
Pasture to Let.
The undersigned at his ranch on the Chowchilla about six miles below Mariposa offers to rent a good pasture well watered, sufficient for a hundred head of stock. For further particulars inquire at this office, L. A. Monroe."[221]

It could be that Louis and Mary, now in their mid-sixties, were ready to ease into a more passive means of income from their property. Well over a century later, at the time of this writing, the land continues to be used for cattle grazing.

That August, George transported yet another illustrious passenger to Yosemite, an experience that carried with it a poignant echo of Grant's visit six years before. Sir Arthur Sullivan, who composed the music to W. S. Gilbert's operettas and several famous religious works, was in Los Angeles and had set aside time to visit Yosemite with several of his family.

Taking an overnight train fourteen hours from Los Angeles to Madera through the searing heat of California's central valley, the party boarded an early morning stage to begin the nine-hour ride to Wawona. Sullivan described it succinctly in his diary: "miserable journey."

John L. Sullivan and Sir Arthur Sullivan

His niece described an incident that took place before reaching Fresno Flats (Oakhurst), possibly near the mining camp of Coarse Gold Gulch. A large group of men surrounded the stage, demanding to see Sullivan. When Sir Arthur made himself known, the men objected, saying "You're not Mr. Sullivan—we want John L. Sullivan!" John L. Sullivan was the heavyweight boxing champion. The men had traveled from far and wide having heard that Sullivan was coming through on the stage, only to find that they had the wrong Sullivan. His niece reported that "they took their disappointment good naturedly."

After a night's stay at the Wawona Hotel, the party traveled into Yosemite. Ben Truman wrote that Monroe had been one of the drivers assigned to transport Sullivan, following the same route connecting Wawona and Yosemite Valley as with Grant's visit, rolling past the same little chapel that Grant had viewed six years before. The next day, Sullivan was invited to attend a 4 p.m. special service at the Yosemite Chapel. It would be a memorial for Grant, who had died sixteen days before, and whose funeral was taking place that same Saturday, August 8, in New York. Sullivan wrote in his diary that he played the organ at the service, and it is perhaps beyond speculation that he would have performed his composition, "Onward Christian Soldiers," in honor of the illustrious fallen warrior.[222]

George Monroe could feel confident about the stability of his employers' business; the Washburn brothers' empire under Henry's direction continued to grow. In February 1886 Washburn's Yosemite Stage & Turnpike Co. finished and opened a new road, engineered by John Conway, trimming 13 miles of travel from the Madera-Yosemite route and replacing the 1870 road built by Samuel Fisher, Galen Clark, and company.[223] In April, Henry Washburn scored another triumph with the opening of a foothill railroad spur ending at a terminal called Raymond, erasing several hours of stage travel from the route to Wawona and Yosemite.[224]

Over the next few decades, Henry Washburn would carry the Yosemite Stage & Turnpike Company into the twentieth century; his brothers, Ed and John, would oversee the transition from horse-drawn stages to motorized "auto-stages," and John's son, Clarence, as manager of the Wawona Hotel in 1934, would celebrate the sixtieth anniversary of Henry Washburn's purchase of the business from Galen Clark.

Everything was in place for a bright future for the Monroes. George's career as a stage driver was secure. Every winter, when Yosemite roads were closed, George likely divided his time between training horses for the stage company and helping out on the family ranch that he might someday inherit. The farm provided subsistence and income that promised to continue well into Mary's and Louis' twilight years.

Chapter VIII

ADVERSITY—*Death of George Monroe. Louis and Mary list their ranch for sale. Mary wins a real-estate lawsuit. Louis dies from a carriage accident.*

The triumph of Mary A. Monroe was complete. From an unpromising future in the pre-war South, through a tumultuous migration to California, Mary had shepherded her family to such a secure position that it inspired the admiration of the local press. And her son had reached the height of his fame.

Just before the middle of November 1886, George Monroe had some trouble while riding a recalcitrant mule, probably near where he lived and worked in Yosemite Valley. According to one account, the mule had thrown Monroe to the ground and then rolled over him. Monroe nursed his injuries for a few days, but his symptoms worsened. On November 15th, unable to drive, he was placed on a makeshift bed in his own stage and ambulanced by another driver to Wawona. At one point along the road, the driver lost control of the stage, but the sound of Monroe's voice calling out from behind the driver calmed the horses.

After a few days, nursed in one of the rooms at the Wawona Hotel, around November 18th Monroe asked to be taken to his parents' ranch. Helped out to the stage, probably carried on a stretcher, Monroe reportedly sensed that he might not survive his injuries. Watching the familiar white railing of the Wawona Hotel recede from his vision, hearing the familiar rattle of the stage and hoof-fall of his beloved horses, George Monroe embarked on a long, painful stage ride down to Pea Ridge. At the home-place built by his parents on the Monroe ranch, George lingered for a short while longer, soothed by the care and the voices of his mother and father.

Then, according to the *Gazette*:

"DIED. — At Monroe's Ranch. Chowchilla, Mariposa county, November 22nd, George F. Monroe aged 42 [*sic*] years."[225]

He was actually only 39 years old. In the same issue of the *Gazette*, an obituary outlines the particulars:

"DEATH OF GEORGE F. MONROE.

The never welcome, but none the less inevitable visitor, Death, has again made his appearance in our community and with but slight warning laid his icy hand upon one whose familiar face and form will be long and well remembered.

George F. Monroe, the subject of this notice, was a native of Georgia, and a son of Mr. and Mrs. L. A. Monroe. His father came to California early in the fifties, locating first in Calaveras county, and thence removing to Mariposa in 1854. His mother arrived the following year, leaving George, (then about 11 years of age) [*sic*, 7 years of age] at school in Washington D.C. A year later he accompanied his uncle to California, coming direct to Mariposa. As a boy he was civil, polite, studious and industrious. As he grew to manhood he tired of the monotony of town life, and developing a natural taste for horsebreaking, riding and driving team, he entered the employment of A. H. WASHBURN & CO., as a Yo Semite guide in 1866 [*sic*, probably 1867].

In 1868 [*sic*, probably 1869] he commenced driving stage for the same company and was in their service up to the date of his illness which was only a few days duration. He left the Valley on the 15th inst., for Wawona, and two or three days later for the home of his parents on Pea Ridge, where he died on Monday last. He had been complaining for some time past

160

and in coming out of the Valley the stage in which he was riding upset by a runaway. He may have received some internal injury from the shock, though he was on his feet in an instant and instinctively sprang to the heads of the leaders and assisted the driver in disentangling the horses and righting the stage.

His funeral took place on Wednesday last from the Methodist Church, and his remains were followed to their earthly resting place by a large concourse of friends.

George was a universal favorite among those who knew him [in] boyhood, as well as hundreds of stranger tourist[s] whom he has guided and conveyed to and from Yo Semite Valley. He was kind, attentive and obliging to all with whom he came in contact, and many a tourist has visited Yo Semite, who came specially consigned to the care of 'George Monroe' by friends who had preceded them over the road. He has also been frequently remembered in complimentary letters and occasionally by substantial tokens of gratitude and esteem.

The duties of the driver of a six horse stage on a mountain road are arduous and responsible. They require a quick eye, a skillful hand, a steady nerve and a peculiar knowledge of horses. George possessed all these qualities to a remarkable degree. His employers say of him "he never met with any accident, never failed to be on time and never cost the company a quarter of a dollar for damages to passengers, horses or vehicles. Whenever George was on the box and held the lines, we knew everything was all right. He always did his duty.

Can any man do more? To his parents he was a dutiful son, as a child, and in manhood a comfort, solace and support to their declining years. The grief-stricken couple have the sympathy of their entire circle of friends and acquaintances."[226]

161

Writer Ben C. Truman recalled:

"The last days of Monroe cast sadness among all who knew him. He had driven daily between Wawona and the Valley every season for many years without an accident of any kind. No obstacle in the way of a fallen tree, fire or sliding rock ever deterred or dismayed him. He knew his horses so well, and they knew him so well, that they would do anything he asked them to do, and many a time he has taken them carefully over a fallen tree two feet or more in diameter, without injury to animal, harness or vehicle. Thousands of people have telegraphed to reserve seats on his stage or have staid over at Wawona to drive with him. He was dangerously, I may say mortally injured, at last while riding a fractious mule that threw him and rolled over on him. The next day he was placed on a bed made in his own stage, drawn by his own six horses, which, by the way, became unmanageable or partly so at the hands of a new driver, until George drew himself up, although in dreadful pain, and talked them out of their disorder. When he arrived at Wawona, the Washburns lifted him out of the stage and put him in one of the best rooms of their hotel, and gave him as much care and medical aid as if he were one of their family. He was in great pain, but all he said was: 'I've driven for the last time, but don't tell my mother.' In a few days, however, he became impatient to be taken to his mother, and was carried down to Mariposa, where he died in her arms in a few hours. ... he was ... an especial favorite with tourists, [and] was greatly liked by the other drivers; and Fort Monroe, between Chinquapin and Inspiration Point, is named after him."[227]

Truman's account of the mule incident helps to explain the *Gazette* report that Monroe "had been complaining for some time past" before the incident with the stage, and explains why Monroe was a passenger instead of the driver. Truman's story also underscores the importance that stage drivers use horses trained to recognize their voices (as mentioned earlier). Though the *Gazette* has the stage "upset by a runaway" and Monroe "on his feet in an instant ... disentangling the horses and righting the stage," Truman's sober and more plausible account has Monroe painfully raising himself to calm his horses and prevent an accident.

George's funeral would have been conducted by Rev. J. T. Murrish, who had just started his one-year residence at the Methodist church in Mariposa. The little church was on the hillside above Main Street, at Fifth Street and Bullion, just a couple blocks from where George had started his career at the Mammoth Tree Livery Stable. After the service, the processional of a "large concourse of friends" would have about a mile to traverse as they followed George Monroe on his sad, final wagon ride to the Mariposa Cemetery.[228]

It is unimaginable that there would not have been a suitable monument placed on his grave, but today the final resting place of George Monroe is unmarked and unknown.

It was possibly not until after George's death that Fort Monroe was named in his honor. Located on the original Wawona Road in Yosemite National Park, uphill from the present road, Fort Monroe was one of several way stations at which stages could change horses. It was near the "Hermitage," referred to earlier in this book. The earliest reference to Fort Monroe found by the author dates from 1890. Theories about the use of "Fort" in the place name range from the unsupported notion that Monroe had a penchant for things military, to the idea that the station may have been used as a checkpoint when the U.S. military administered Yosemite before the establishment of the National Park Service in 1916. The latter theory is weakened by the fact that Fort Monroe was so called for at least a year before the military took control of the park. It seems possible, though, that the tribute to George Monroe may also acknowledge a site by the same name that holds a deep significance in African American history. Construction of the first Fort Monroe in the U.S. began in Virginia in 1819 at a place called Point Comfort, where in 1619 the first enslaved Africans arrived on the coast, and where in 1861 enslaved people would come seeking liberation, referring to the Union army outpost as "Freedom's Fortress."[229]

On Yosemite's Glacier Point Road in a reference from 1885, "Monroe Gap" appears in conjunction with Badger Pass, giving evidence that George Monroe had been honored with at least one place name during his short lifetime. Still identified on current maps, "Monroe Meadow" shares its location with Badger Pass, which became Yosemite's downhill ski area in 1935.[230]

One week after their son's death, the grieving parents published this in the *Gazette*:

"A CARD.

Mr. and Mrs. L. A. Monroe take this method of expressing their thanks to the many friends of their only son, George, for the kind assistance rendered them in their great bereavement. It is a ray of comfort to them in their declining years, to know that their beloved son carried with him the high esteem of a host of friends."[231]

A week after that, on December 11th, Louis and Mary listed their ranch for sale:

164

Monroe Ranch site (Author photograph)

"FOR SALE.
A FARM RANCH, CONSISTING OF 480
Acres, well-watered and well-timbered, is offered for sale by
the undersigned. Said Ranch is situated about five miles
below Mariposa, with good wagon road leading out to all the
principal towns and places. There is excellent pasturage at
the present time, besides a large percentage of tillable land,
several springs of water and everything necessary to make it
a magnificent home. For a dairy ranch, for from fifty to
seventy-five cows it has no superior. The country on three
sides is open Government land, which makes it decidedly
favorable to its owner for a stock ranch. The whole ranch is
enclosed by a fence. The oak timber is fair to split and make
rails. A good dwelling house with pantry kitchen and
cupboards already built and in order, besides a smoke and
meat house; and lastly, but equally important, a good barn

and stable for your horses. A great deal can be said in favor of this ranch for the purposes of a home, raising stock and making a comfortable living for a family. For further particulars, apply to L. A. MONROE or to Angevine Reynolds, Editor of this paper."[232]

The Monroes may have already considered selling the ranch, given how soon they had listed it in the wake of their son's death. They were probably eager to retire from ranching and live off of their savings. Around this time Mary's brother, George Millen, closed down his blacksmith shop on the Monroe property and moved to Southern California. By the next year, Millen reopened his blacksmithing business in the Logan Heights area of San Diego, California, where he would spend the rest of his life. In December 1886, Mary recorded a new homestead claim at the county recorder's office, taking possession of the property that her son had homesteaded the previous January.[233]

The Christmas Day edition of the *Gazette* values the Monroe ranch at $4,800 (currently equaling $154,000):

"The ranch of L. A. Monroe, which is advertised in this paper and offered for sale, is one of the most desirable offered in this county. For an industrious man with a family no better can be found in the foothills. For a dairy business there is good pasturage nearly the whole year round. It is well watered with springs, besides there are several thousand cords of wood, which is within reach of a market at $6 per cord. The land is not too hilly and soil equally fertile and productive to any in the county. This certainly is the most attractive and profitable piece of land of 480 acres we know of for sale. It possesses good improvements and can be bought for $10 per acre. No better land for grape raising is selling in Fresno to-day from 25 to 50 dollars per acre."[234]

But the Monroes' plans were soon derailed. In 1887 two neighbors, William Grove and David Allen made an illegal real estate transaction involving 180 acres of Mary Monroe's property. Grove, aged 40, a Virginian and Confederate veteran of the Civil War, had recently run a stamp mill for his uncle, a very successful local miner named John Hite. Allen, 63, was a local constable, born in Alabama. According to court documents, in May 1887 Grove had somehow obtained from a local Justice Court a judgment against Mary Monroe's right of ownership of her property. The next month, constable Allen, apparently claiming ownership of Mary's land, proceeded to sell the property to Grove. [235]

Ten months later, in April 1888 Mary filed suit against the neighbors, claiming in part that they:

" … went through the form of purchasing the said real estate with full notice thereof, and desiring to injure and oppress the plaintiff and put her to great and unnecessary trouble and expense … whereby the plaintiff has been and is greatly injured and disunified."[236]

Why it had taken ten months for Mary to bring the issue to court is unknown. Possibly she hadn't learned of the transaction until a potential buyer may have discovered irregularities in the title documents. Additionally, it would take time to make the final critical decision to sue, prepare the case, and then schedule a court date.

Grove and Allen would be represented in court by the Mariposa District Attorney, Newman Jones. Mary's attorney was Joseph Whipple Congdon, a distinguished biologist out of Stanford University who also practiced law. As an attorney,

167

according to a later article, "he was more keenly interested in the science of the profession than its actual practice," but he "earned the cognomen of 'The Honest Lawyer' because of a discriminating sense of justice and integrity shown in every case with which he was connected." [237]

2

That plaintiffs declaration of Homestead made Dec. 13, 1886, was valid and in full force at time of the levy of the execution by defendant D. P. Allen and at time of sale mentioned in findings of fact and still is in full force

3

That the sale mentioned in the findings of fact was illegal and the certificate of sale issued by defendant D. P. Allen to defendant Wm. G. Grove was issued contrary to law and is a cloud upon plaintiffs title.

4

That plaintiff is entitled to a judgment and decree as prayed for in her complaint and to her costs and to a dismissal of the cross-complaint.

Decree and judgment ordered in conformity with the above

John M. Corcoran
Judge

May 10th 1888.

Last page of Mariposa District Court judgment in favor of Mary A. Monroe
(Mariposa Museum and History Center Collection)

Mary won her case on May 10, 1888. According to the statement issued by Judge John M. Corcoran:

> … both defendants before the aforesaid sale of said property on the 28th of June 1887 had notice of the existence of the land … and also knew that plaintiff and her husband resided on said land.

> " … plaintiff's declaration of Homestead made Dec. 13, 1886 was valid and in full force at … time of sale mentioned in findings of fact and still is in full force.

> … the sale mentioned in the findings of fact was illegal and the certificate of sale … was issued contrary to law and is a cloud upon plaintiff's title."

> … plaintiff is entitled to a judgment and decree as prayed for in her complaint and to her costs and to a dismissal of the cross-complaint.[238]

Though Mary won in court, the controversy had been devastating for the bereft Monroes. The "cloud upon the plaintiff's title," due to the contested ownership, would have stalled any attempt to sell the property until the issue was resolved. Now, after two years of inaction, the Monroes had reclaimed clear, uncontested title to their property, and could finally resume their plan to sell the ranch.

But only three months after Mary's court victory, when the land was thoroughly parched under the August sun, another blow was delivered to the Monroes:

"FIRES.
… [A] fire, which broke out on Saturday, near old man Hoskin's residence, on Mariposa creek, about two miles

below Mormon Bar, made its way across the country in a southeasterly direction, destroying in its course a portion of Frank Mello's fence, and from thence to L. A. Monroe's ranch, where, we understand, it done considerable damage, by the destruction of a long string of fence which enclosed his pasturage and cultivated fields. But for the timely aid of some neighbors, Mr. and Mrs. Monroe's comfortable home, consisting of a dwelling house, barn and farming utensils, with which they are well supplied, would all have been destroyed …. As a matter of precaution, especially about a home, a barrel kept filled with water and buckets close by should be made a matter of necessity …."[239]

Fortunately, the aging Monroes had many good friends and neighbors and through their efforts, the fire was prevented from obliterating the Monroes' last prospects for a secure future. Still, there was plenty of damage. The loss of the fence would impact their ability to earn income through the leasing of pasturage. For Louis, who was already in declining health, it was doubtful whether he could rebuild the fence or plant a new crop the following year.

Over the next two years, the Monroes most likely subsisted off of the fruits of their ranch and farm that, having lost much of its fencing, failed even more so to attract a buyer. Then in March 1890, misfortune struck yet again:

"Last Tuesday as Mr. and Mrs. L. A. Munroe [sic] were coming into town from their ranch, they encountered a big rock somewhere in the road and in the efforts of their wheels to dislodge it, overturned their wagon, throwing both occupants out among the rocks, severely bruising them. Fortunately, no bones were broken …. The road from their ranch to town is very narrow and rocky, and should the road

170

be built from Raymond, some hard work will have to be done on this part of it, to render it travelable."[240]

Six days later the delayed result of their accident brought an appalling, tragic echo of their son's death:

"DIED.
MUNROE [*sic*]—At Red Mountain, May 24th, 1890, Louis Augustus Monroe, a native of Georgia, aged 70 years."[241]

"Death of Louis A. Munroe.
The death of Louis A. Munroe, the well-known colored man of that name, removes another old settler of Mariposa county. Coming here, in the fifties as a free man, with his wife, he carried on the business of a barber, on Main street, for a number of years, residing in town. After awhile he took up the ranch, on which he lived for many years, about six miles south-east of Mariposa, where by industry and perseverance he succeeded in making one of the finest ranches in the county. Mr. Munroe leaves no children. His only son, George, who was favorably known to the traveling public in Europe, as well as this country, as one of the most skillful and trusted stage-drivers of the Yosemite Stage lines, preceded him to the grave by several years. Mr. Munroe's health has been failing for sometime, but his death was hastened by the accident of being thrown out of a wagon some weeks ago. He was buried in the Mariposa graveyard, and his funeral was attended by quite a number of our older residents."[242]

As in the case of his son, the location of Louis Monroe's grave within the Mariposa Cemetery remains unknown.

Just four years after everything was so promising for her family, Mary found herself alone, 68 years old, living on a huge

171

ranch that was losing money. At some point she had taken out a mortgage on the ranch, perhaps to make improvements, expecting to pay it off upon the sale of the property. Another year passed, and sometime in the summer of 1891, Mary had run through her savings.

That September, the *Gazette* announced foreclosure proceedings against Mary A. Monroe. Unable to find a buyer for the property, unable to make the payments on a mortgage valued at $2,422 — about half the value of the property — she would see her hard-earned beautiful ranch auctioned off to the highest bidder the following month.[243]

Mary somehow managed to stay in the area for the next three years. Finally, she made the hard decision to leave Mariposa and headed south to join her brother in San Diego. Duly reported in the *Gazette* in May 1894:

> "Mrs. M. A. Monroe has left Mariposa after a residence of thirty-five years, and has gone to Southern California to make a new home."[244]

SAN DIEGO—*Mary joins her brother in San Diego. The death of Mary Monroe. George Millen testifies at the Coroner's inquest.*

Assisted once again by George Millen, who had shown his sister the way from Georgia to California forty years earlier, Mary, in her mid-seventies, embarked on a new life in an unfamiliar place. According to the *San Diego Union*:

> "[George] applied to Mrs. Harriet Bailey, who kept a lodging house near Ninth and K streets, for a room for his sister, who was daily expected from Merced .... After a few months spent

172

at Mrs. Bailey's lodging house, Mrs. Monroe went to Alpine to work as a domestic, later entering the employ of Col. John Kastle."[245]

George had pointed out in his testimony that Mary "never knew what it was to work for families or anybody else until she came to this [area]." It was in 1896 that Mary took up residence with the Kastles in San Diego. The Kastles would later assert that, due to Mary's light complexion, they had believed Mary was White.

Working for the first time in her life as a servant, and for a couple self-described as being "from slave states" but unaware of her African heritage, Mary must have felt keenly the sad irony of her situation.[246]

Mary left the employ of the Kastles in September 1897:

"Mrs. Monroe was a widow, about 63 [*sic* actually 75] years old, and up to three months ago was employed as a domestic by Col. John Kastle at No 35 Eighteenth street. On account of failing health, she left three months ago to live in a cottage on Main street, where she expected to make a living by raising chickens."[247]

With her final paycheck of $100 from Col. Kastle, Mary took up residence at 611 Main Street, between 30th and 31st on the north side of the street. Among her possessions were:

" ... a Wheeler & Wilson sewing machine in fairly good condition, a pair of opera glasses, two trunks with quite a large quantity of underwear, and other articles, such as books, pictures and so on ... a lot of wearing apparel hanging on the wall in one of the rooms, a coal-oil stove, a large quantity of cooking utensils, tinware, and some small quantity of provisions, partly in the kitchen and partly found in a box standing in the other room, and a water-barrel, outside."[248]

It could be that Mary, remembering the cautionary words in the *Mariposa Gazette* after her ranch burned eight years before, continued to keep a filled water barrel outside for emergencies as well as utility. Now living on her own, unemployed, in failing health, and short of funds, Mary once again found herself in dire circumstances. It was around the first of November, 1897, that Mary made a two-mile trip to visit her brother at his home and blacksmith shop on K Street between 9th and 10th. It would be their last visit together. George recalled:

"She was to my place of business about two weeks ago, as near as I can guess. She called in one evening and spoke to me and told me her condition was very poor, and that she thought of getting another place where she could raise chickens, and I told her I was sorry I was not able to help her, there was a time I had been, but at the present time I was not able to help her. I have been financially and physically oppressed, and mentally."

Mary then wrote to a recently established benevolent institution called the *Helping Hand Home and Mission* at the corner of 5th and J St., which offered a temporary home for the unemployed. She referred to them in a note addressed to a Mrs. Dodson at Mr. Dodson's real estate office. Though Mary sent the note on the thirteenth, it wouldn't reach its destination until the day after her death:

"Dear Mrs Dodson. I dropped a line to the Helping Hand a few days ago of my sad condition, not able to work and not

174

enough to eat. Oh do not let me starve to death. Yours, M.A. Munroe [*sic*], Main street N. 611. I took cold and it fell on my nerves, I walk but slow."[249]

On Sunday the fourteenth of November 1897, Mary's former employers, John and Mrs. Kastle, drove out in a buggy to visit her:

" … she said she was poor. She complained of having no means, to different persons. [Under our employ] we paid her a good deal of money and we thought she ought to have some. We paid her, I guess, in the neighborhood of $100 the last time she was with us …. We always paid her every week promptly."

After her visitors had left, Mary, hungry and frail, selected a warm coat from a peg on the wall and began a laborious six-block walk north to National Ave., where she left this note with the druggist:

"San Diego. Please send the water man to 611 Main street."

Mary had experience with long, arduous treks. From Georgia to Calaveras County was one thing for a young woman, but in her present condition, the six blocks home in the dark would be daunting. Instead of heading south toward her home using 30th St., Mary chose to walk east on National, perhaps with the intention to make a right turn heading south on 31st, then another right heading west on Main to her cottage. There would be no point in boarding the electric street car on National since its terminus was only a block east at 31st St.

It was nearing 6 p.m. on a cold, dark autumn evening. Mary moved slowly, deliberately, head bowed down, following the National Avenue streetcar tracks on her right. Having traversed about 85 feet, in an instant Mary Monroe passed into history.

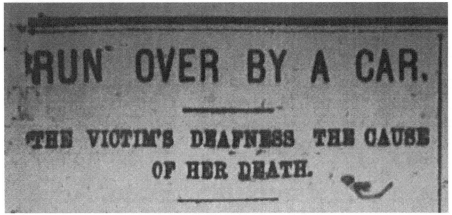

San Diego Union, November 15, 1897

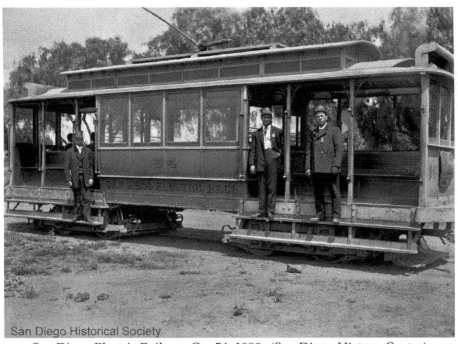

San Diego Electric Railway Car 54, 1890s (San Diego History Center)

J. D. Rogers, motorman for the San Diego Electric Railway Company, was also heading east, handling the controls of Car No. 3. Rogers described what happened:

"I forget whether it was her right foot or left, I think it was her right foot was just going over the rail when I seen her. Coming up behind my head light, you see, I could not see the woman, but just as soon as she stepped in the light I seen her. It was very dark, cloudy, if you remember .... Her back was towards me and she never looked up from the time I hollered. I hollered at her twice. I hollered just before the car struck her, and just as she went to step in the track. She never looked up at all, just looked right at the ground, and she never made a noise of any kind when the car struck her at all .... I grabbed my controller handle with one hand and my reverse with the other. I brought my controller handle back to about the sixth notch, and throwed my reverse the other way, reversed the car ... just as soon as I got my car stopped, I just turned around and told them 'My God I have killed a woman.'"

The several witnesses examined by the Coroner established that the driver had acted quickly and correctly. During the investigation, Col. John Kastle (quoted earlier) testified extensively to Monroe's deafness and her character, and that he'd been unaware, due to Mary's light complexion, that she was African American. Kastle, aged 64, was a real estate investor and developer who had been president of the San Diego Chamber of Commerce and had once run for mayor of that city. He described Mary Monroe at her work:

"Well, sir, people could come to the door there where she was at work right at the kitchen table, right this way (indicating) and the door was over there (indicating) and she would be turned the other way, and they could knock the door down and she would not hear them. They could rattle, rattle just as much as they pleased, she would not hear them if she was looking the other way, cooking or doing anything about the sink in any way, within ten feet, yes within eight feet of the door, she would not hear anybody if they were knocking. The baker soon found out that she could not hear and he would come right in. She got in the habit of laying the ticket down on the table and he would come in and lay the bread down and go off ...."

Kastle went on to describe her as:

" ... not strong, but very active .... Smart as anybody in every way, smart intellectually, a fine old lady, a very nice old woman ... the smartest old lady I ever saw."

George Millen's lucid account of his family's history might have been enough to establish his identity as Mary's only surviving relative, but there remained another question. To the Coroner and his jurors, Mary did not appear to be African American, while George Millen did. The Coroner and jury members, showing their uncertainty about Mary's race, subjected her brother to an uncomfortable grilling on the subject of skin complexion. During the session, one of the jurors is at first confused by Millen's use of analogy, but Millen shows restraint and patience with his questioners as he deftly explains his stance:

"Q. How do you account for her [Mary] being so fair?

A. Well, I will tell you. I see it every day. You will have me explain it to you, sir?

Q. If you please.

A. We see every day Mexicans come here with a family of children, one light, and two or three colored, dark—now if you will explain that to me, I will acknowledge it.

A JUROR: Do you claim to be a Mexican?

WITNESS: No sir, I claim to be an American, sir—I do not claim it, it is simply a fact.

THE JUROR: Born in Georgia makes you an American.

Q. Was your father a full blooded negro?

A. Negro? Well, if he was I do not know it. Do you know anything about it? I have asked the question a hundred times. That is all that hurts my popularity here, that I cannot get down and say I am a negro. My father was a man, my mother a lady, and I do not know nothing more. I have never saw anybody that was blacker than me—if I was blacker than the hinges of hell I would get up and tell you—and if we stood on a level we would be just on a level.

Q. Was your father as dark as you are?

A. I think he was about my complexion.

Q. Was your mother darker or lighter?

A. My mother was a shade lighter than me, I think.

Q. How were the other children?

A. Three dark and three light.

Q. Were any of them as light as this sister who was dead?

A. Yes, there were none of them darker than me though."

A JUROR: Do you claim to be a Mexican?

WITNESS: No sir, I claim to be an American sir --- I do not claim it, it is simply a fact.

THE JUROR: Born in Georgia makes you an American.

Q Was your father a full blooded negro?   A Negro? Well if he was I do not know it. Do you know anything about it? I have asked the question a hundred times. That is all that hurts my popularity here, that I can not get down and say I am a negro. My father was a man, my mother a lady, and I do not know nothing more. I have never saw anybody that was blacker than me --- if I was blacker than the hinges of hell I would get up and tell you --- and if we stood on a level we would be just on a level.

Q Was your father as dark as you are?   A I think he was about my complexion.

Q Was your mother darker or lighter?   A My mother was a shade lighter than me I think.

Q How were the other children?   A Three dark and three light.

Q Were any of them as light as this sister who was dead? A Yes, there were none of them darker than me though.

Q You knew her when she was a little girl, you say she cared for you?   A No, she knew me when I was a little boy, and when I knew her she was a good big girl, because she could not have nursed me if she hadnt been. There was one between me and her, understand.

Coroner's Inquest, page 47 (San Diego History Center)

A local newspaper summed up the matter:

"Another fact concerning the woman [Mary Monroe] that occasioned surprise yesterday was the appearance at the undertaking parlors where her dead body lies of [George Millen], a colored blacksmith who lives on K street, between Ninth and Tenth, and who identified the body as that of his sister. … a few persons who knew both Millen and the woman … had heard both say that they were brother and sister …."[250]

A public administrator estimated the value of her possessions to be "about twenty-five dollars—enough to pay the funeral expenses of the deceased" (about $900 adjusted to the year 2023). The key to her cottage would be turned over to her brother, who according to a news account "took possession of the premises." A sensationalized account of Mary's death and inquest came out the next day, advancing the notion that Mary's death hadn't been an accident:

"It was learned yesterday that Mrs. Monroe, a few minutes before her death, had left her name and address at the drug store near the scene of the accident, and this has given rise to the suspicion that she intended to commit suicide by throwing herself in front of the car. Her deafness was pronounced, but the headlight in front of the car shone brilliantly on the track far in advance of her before she stepped between the rails and was killed, and this of itself might have served as a warning. Her poverty and advancing age is given by acquaintances as a probable reason for suicide."[251]

Actually, the note referenced in the article was an order for a future water delivery, which controverts the "suspicion that she intended to commit suicide." Whether Mary should have seen the light on the street coming from behind and moved out of the way of the car is left to speculation. But Mary had been investigating her options, such as the Helping Hand mission and reaching out to friends, and her ordering water that very day suggests that Mary planned to continue living, even though faced with some terribly serious issues.

Within forty-eight hours of her death, after the conclusion of the Coroner's Inquest, Mary Monroe was buried on November 16, at Mount Hope Cemetery, two and a half miles from her last home.[252]

Mary A. Monroe had guided her family to a respected place in history. Her son, celebrity stage driver George Frazier Monroe, had died at the height of his and his family's achievements. Her husband, barber, farmer, and civil rights activist Louis Monroe died amid diligent efforts to sell their ranch and secure their future. Mary ended up back with the brother she'd helped raise seventy years before, whose loyalty had in turn helped Mary and her family immeasurably. Of her ending, this much is true: had her brother not invited her to San Diego, had there been no municipal streetcar accident to prompt an inquest and press coverage, and had George not been there to testify, the Monroes' story might have perished with her.

As she labored alongside those tracks, bundled against the cold and clutching her collar with her head down in the darkness, who can say what images were passing through the mind of that "smart old lady." Surely her son was in her thoughts—the eleventh anniversary of his death was only a week away. Perhaps her eyes were closed as her footsteps faltered, slowly, over the street, over the tracks, her deafness blocking out all sounds but those of her memories: a hummed lullaby as she rocked her infant brother in

Georgia, the firm chiff of pen on paper as her husband registered to vote, a cheering crowd in those shining hours when her own son shared his stage with General Grant.

A lone elderly blacksmith, who apparently had never married, George Millen was the sole remaining witness to the full arc of his family's epic journey. He lived another fifteen years, saw the dawn of the automobile era, and at the venerable age of 86 died in San Diego on June 18, 1912. Two days later Millen was buried near his sister at Mount Hope Cemetery—fifty years after he and Louis Monroe left Georgia for the gold fields of California.[253]

All through the nineteenth century, cultural barriers were cracked open through enormous effort, sacrifice, and bloodshed. In lockstep with those efforts, the tenacious Monroes strained through each new opening in pursuit of their dreams.

Wielding the power of those dreams, George Monroe carried forward his family's indomitable spirit, rising through the maelstrom of his era to a place of triumph and hard-earned recognition as *"the greatest of all."*

George Monroe c. 1885 (Yosemite Museum and Archives)[254]

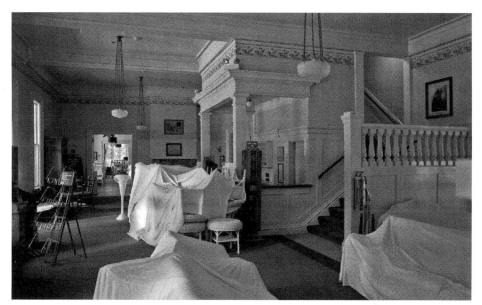

Wawona Hotel Lobby, Winter Closure, 1988 (Author photograph)

Epilogue

The hotel building constructed by George Monroe's employers in 1879 still operates, but every winter the Wawona Hotel closes for a little while. On those snowy nights, as tourists leave Monroe Meadow from a day's skiing in Yosemite, an occasional auto will stray off the Wawona Road to circle the hotel's front drive, headlights casting gossamer patterns across the dark lobby, projected through rippled antique windows.

The fleeting lights reveal a framed photograph on the wall: George Monroe looks with placid confidence across the empty lobby where a memory of Ulysses S. Grant puffs a cigar in front of the fireplace, perceptible only in the imagination. Another headlight image slides across the room. Grant catches Monroe's eye and, as so very long ago under the Big Trees, they smile one of those slow, wise smiles, and say nothing.

CHRONOLOGY

Year	Month	Family History	Collateral History
circa 1794		Birth of George Millen (Sr.) in Pennsylvania, presumed husband of Polly	
circa 1800		Birth of Polly Millen in Pennsylvania	
circa 1811-1820		Birth of Louis Monroe in Georgia	
1814			"Black Refugees" sail from Maryland to Nova Scotia
1820		Millen family residing in Waynesboro, GA	
circa 1821-1824		Millen family move to Ohio and then to Westbury, PA	
circa 1822		Birth of Mary Ann Millen, likely in Ohio	
1822	Apr 27		Birth of Hiram Ulysses Grant (Ulysses S. Grant) in Ohio
circa 1825		Millen family return to Waynesboro from Pennsylvania	
	Aug 9	Birth of George Richard Millen in Georgia	
circa 1834		Death of George Millen (Sr.), presumed husband of Polly	

		Move of Millen family from Waynesboro to Augusta, GA. Around this time George R. Millen adopted by a French family in Augusta	
1847		Approx. move of Polly Millen, Mary A. Millen, and family to Columbus, GA. Approx. marriage of Mary A. Millen and Louis Augustus Monroe. Birth of George Frazier Monroe. George Millen goes to Mexico	
1849			Slavery banned by California Constitution
1850			Thomas Thorn and enslaved workers arrive in Mariposa, possibly including Moses Rodgers
1852		George Millen and Louis Monroe in Calaveras County	
1854		George Millen returns to Columbus, cares for George Monroe while Mary goes to California. George Millen moves to Washington, D.C.; enrolls George Monroe in school	

circa 1855-1856		George Millen brings George Monroe to Mariposa, California	Seth and Ed Washburn in Mariposa area (Bridgeport)
1857			Galen Clark builds cabin at what would become Wawona
1858		Louis Monroe's barbershop likely established in Mariposa by this year, located by the Pine Tree House (hotel & saloon)	
	June	Fire destroys Mariposa business district, displacing Monroe's barbershop	
1859			Henry Washburn arrives in Mariposa area (Bridgeport)
1860		George Millen in Weaverville, CA	
1861	Jan	Louis Monroe's barbershop reopened as the Pine Tree Tonsorial Saloon	
1862		George Monroe finds a "piece of quartz" worth $273.	Passage of Homestead Act
1863		Louis files for homestead but does not follow through	
1864			Yosemite and Mariposa Big Trees Grant passed
1865	Jan		13th Amendment to US Constitution passed, abolishes slavery

	July	Louis Monroe listed as Agent for *The Elevator*	
	Sep 12	"Mass meeting" of African Americans in Mariposa; Louis Monroe chairman	
	Oct 25-27		Moses Rodgers represents Mariposa at "Colored Convention" in Sacramento, CA
	Nov		Henry Washburn partners with John Bruce in mining venture
	Dec		Henry Washburn marries Jean Bruce
1866	April	Fire again destroys Mariposa business district, displacing Louis Monroe's Pine Tree Tonsorial Saloon	
	Dec	Construction begins on Schlageter Hotel, including Louis Monroe's tonsorial service	
1867	Jan 19		Henry Washburn enters Yosemite tourism business with purchase of livery stable in Mariposa
	Mar 16		J. J. Cook newly reported as partner to Washburn
	Mar 20		John Bruce newly reported as partner to Washburn and Cook

		George Monroe hired by Washburn, Bruce, and Cook	
1868			Fourteenth Amendment to US Constitution passed; expands citizenship rights to African Americans without interference from individual states
circa 1869		Death of Polly Millen	
1869			Washburn partners with J. R. McCready. Cook and Bruce no longer appear to be partners with Washburn
1870		Louis Monroe first African American to register to vote in Mariposa County; ranch established under Mary's name	Fifteenth Amendment to US Constitution passed, granting right to vote to African American men
1870-1871			Fisher & Co. competing stage line on Mariposa route. New road connects Mariposa and Clark's, built by Clark and Fisher & Co.
1871			Railroad reaches Merced; Washburn & McCready advertise round-trip tickets from San Francisco to Yosemite

	July 24		Washburn & McCready bring carriage into Yosemite Valley, carry Susan B. Anthony and Elizabeth Cady Stanton
1872		Mary Monroe shown as owning 160 acres at Pea Ridge. In voter registrations George listed as "Teamster." Louis listed as "Rancher" though continuing to work in Mariposa as a barber	
1874		George Monroe stationed in Merced, stage driver for Washburn & McCready	J. J. Cook reappears as San Francisco agent for Washburn & McCready.
	Jun/Jul		Opening of Coulterville Road, then Big Oak Flat Road into Yosemite
	Aug 12		John McCready dies (Henry Washburn's partner)
	Nov 2		"Clark's bridge" (Wawona Covered Bridge) "in process of construction"
	Dec 9		Road from Clark's to Yosemite Valley under construction
	Dec 22		Washburn purchase of Clark & Moore's

1875	April		Clark & Moore's renamed Big Tree Station by this time
	May	Congressional member James A. Garfield visits Yosemite (George Monroe, driver)	
	July 22		Grand opening of Mariposa Road
		George Monroe assigned to Mariposa Road	
circa 1876		George Monroe residence changes from Mariposa to Merced	Construction of "Long White" (now "Clark Cottage") at Big Tree Station by Joseph Shelly
1877		Louis Monroe moves his barbering business to J.H. Miller's Capital Saloon on 5th & Main, Mariposa	John Bruce reappears as partner to Washburn with J. J. Cook as investor
	Mar 8		Henry Washburn listed as principal owner of Big Tree Station after buying previous partners' half-ownership and other assets for $20,000
1878	Nov 30		Fire destroys Big Tree Station, Long White (now Clark Cottage) spared
1879	April 1	This year, George Monroe residence changes from Merced to Yosemite Valley	First guests (10 persons) of season arrive at Big Tree Station; probably housed in Long

193

			White while Main Building still under construction
	April 5		Road from Fresno Flats (now Oakhurst) to Big Tree Station under construction
	May		Road to and through Mariposa Grove under construction
	May 2		Opening of road from Fresno Flats (now Oakhurst) to Big Tree Station
	June 5		Possible opening of new Main Building at Big Tree Station
	June 7		New Mariposa Brass Band performing under Thomas H. DeVall
	Oct 1		Ulysses S. Grant takes stage from Madera to Big Tree Station
	Oct 2	George Monroe drives Grant from Big Tree Station to Yosemite Valley	
	Oct 5	Monroe drives Grant from Yosemite Valley to Big Tree Station for lunch, then to Mariposa Grove and back to Big Tree Station	
	Oct 6		Grant departs Big Tree Station via Mariposa

1880		Rutherford B. Hayes visits Yosemite (George Monroe, driver)	
1882		William T. Sherman visits Yosemite (George Monroe, driver)	
	Mar 4		Death of John Bruce
1883		Charles A. Dana visits Yosemite (George Monroe, driver)	
1884		George Millen moves to Monroe Ranch as blacksmith. Lillie Langtry visits Yosemite (George Monroe, driver)	
	Jan		Announcement that "Big Tree Station has been changed to Wawona."
1885	Aug	Sir Arthur Sullivan visits Wawona; George Monroe transports him to Yosemite Valley; Sullivan plays organ in Yosemite Chapel for Grant's memorial	
1886	Feb		New road built by John Conway trims 13 miles from the Madera-Yosemite route
	April 5		Railroad terminus at the new town of Raymond established
	Nov 22	Death of George Monroe	

	Dec 25	Monroe Ranch listed for sale	
		George Millen moves to San Diego	
1887	May - Jun	Illegal transaction clouds title to Monroe property	
1888	May 10	Mary wins real estate lawsuit in Mariposa court, clears title on Monroe Ranch	
	Aug 11	Fire damages much of Monroe Ranch	
1890	May 24	Death of Louis Monroe six days after carriage accident	
1891	Oct	Monroe Ranch foreclosure auction	
1894	May 26	Mary Monroe moves to San Diego	
1897	Nov 14	Death of Mary A. Monroe	
	Nov 16	Coroner's Inquest	
1912	June 18	Death of George Millen	

NOTES

Primary sources are given to support the subject of this history, while non-primary sources are used to support general background history. Online sources are intended as an aid to readers seeking further information and wider confirmation on the various subjects presented here. Internet addresses available at this printing will likely expire over time; readers are encouraged to search online for updated and new sources after the ones listed become obsolete.

---

[1] *Mariposa Gazette*, November 27, 1897, pg. 1, col. 1, 2, 4. James McCauley is reported as "quietly circulating around Mariposa" after his ouster from Yosemite, which had been reported two weeks earlier (*Mariposa Gazette*, November 13, 1897, pg. 1, col. 2).

[2] My guess as to the moon's phase and position that evening derived from astropixels.com - this site currently offers dates of moon phases in the 1800s.

[3] Signal Peak (aka Devil Peak) is visible on the horizon, in line vertically with the left side of the dirt road. Also visible from Wawona, the mountain serves as a geographical fulcrum between the Monroe Ranch and George Monroe's future base of employment.

[4] *Mariposa Gazette*, November 27, 1886, pg. 3-4, col. 3.

[5] (Turner 1959): 116.

[6] All of George Millen's words come from the *San Diego Coroner's Inquest No. 524*, November 16, 1897; copy in the San Diego History Center Research Archives, filed under: PR 2.69–F113–2–Coroner #524, Box 15/22. The *Inquest* is a word-for-word transcript of the Coroner's and jurors' questions and witnesses' answers. As a result of this format, the storyline of each witness's testimony comes out fragmented by questions, and out of chronological order as facts are remembered and disclosed. Excerpts from the *Coroner's Inquest* have been arranged by the author to reconstruct the testimony into a chronological narrative.

Portions of the Coroner's Inquest were published in Palmer, Barbara. 2001, "None Darker Than Me: Racial obsession in 19th-century San Diego;" *San Diego Weekly Reader* currently online at sandiegoreader.com/news/2001/aug/02/cover-none-darker-me/ (accessed 3/21/2023).

[7] "Mrs. Bell" is probably a mis-transcription; *San Diego Union*, November 16, 1897 identifies the lodging-house keeper as Mrs. Harriet Bailey.

Genealogical notes: Millen testified to the Coroner that he was the only "near relative:" "Only near—she has got a niece, she has several nieces in Colorado. I have a brother that died there fifty years ago." Millen also testified when asked if Mary had any children, "One child, sir—had two, but one lived and the other died."

[8] The birth year for George Richard Millen appears on his burial record as August 9, 1825, and is corroborated by the U.S. Census Bureau for years 1860, 1900 (which also give his birth-month as August), 1910, and voter registrations from 1872, 1887, and 1894.

Overview of the circumstances affecting the Millen family at that time and place: (Free Blacks in the Antebellum Period 1998).

[9] With George Millen's well-documented birth-year of 1825, and knowing that another sibling was born after Mary and before George's birth, George's statement brings into question the accuracy of other documents giving Mary's birth-year. Various records, including any in the possession of the Coroner's office, showed Mary as being younger than George—not older. On one hand, the 1880 census puts Mary's birth as 1830 in Ohio, and Louis' (her husband) as 1820 in Georgia, but the 1850 census shows a discrepancy by instead putting Mary's birth as 1825 in Georgia, and Louis' as 1817 in Georgia. George provides the most plausible testimony to Mary's birth year as 1822.

[10] A description of Kentucky's Underground Railroad is currently available on the website of Kentucky Educational Television at: ket.org/education/resources/kentuckys-underground-railroad-passage-freedom (accessed 3/21/2023).

[11] (Free Blacks in the Antebellum Period 1998).

[12] (Slave to Free," The Making of African American Identity, Vol. 1, 1500–1865 2009); and (Smith 2011); and (Baumgartner 2020).

[13] (Jordan 2007).

Two previous censuses (1850 and 1870) list Mary's birthplace as Georgia. The 1880 census entry stands out in its contradiction of those entries, giving Ohio as her birthplace and including her parents' birthplace of Pennsylvania. It appears possible that the contradiction was not an accident; 1880 finds Mary at her most confident, and perhaps most inclined to set down an accurate account of her origins—though she still understated her age. Contradicting Mary's 1880 placement of her mother's birthplace as Pennsylvania, the census in 1850 gives Polly's birthplace as South Carolina, and in 1870 as Georgia. Though Mary's 1880 account may be the most compelling, the question of her and her parents' birthplaces remains in question until corroborative evidence surfaces.

[14] (Thomas 2019).

Regarding Westbury, a lesser possibility remains that the "Westbury" referred to by George Millen was not in Pennsylvania but rather the one in New York, 40 miles from New York Harbor and a link in the Underground Railroad. Information on Westbury, NY can be found online currently at sites such as this: womenhistoryblog.com/2015/06/underground-railroad-on-long-island.html (accessed 3/21/2023). There also currently appears to be a "Westbury" neighborhood about 100 miles west of Augusta, GA, associated with the town of Watkinsville, GA, but appearing to lack any historical associations.

[15] "List of Letters Remaining in the Post Office in Waynesborough," *The Georgia Constitutionalist*, July 11, 1834 (Augusta, Ga.), listing "Polly Millen," currently available courtesy Digital Library of Georgia, Georgia Historic Newspapers at: gahistoricnewspapers.galileo.usg.edu/lccn/sn90052030/1834-07-11/ed-1/seq-4 (accessed 3/21/2023).

[16] A discussion of French families in Georgia is currently available courtesy the New Georgia Encyclopedia at: georgiaencyclopedia.org/articles/history-archaeology/french-presence-georgia (accessed 3/21/2023).

[17] (African Nova Scotians in the Age of Slavery and Abolition, Black Refugees, 1813-1834. 2023).

[18] Photograph title "Old log slave cabin - 'D' on diagram - Sotterly, Slave Quarters, State Route 245 and Vista Road Vicinity, Hollywood, St. Mary's County, MD," Douglas Barber, photographer, c. 1933. Current location Library of Congress Prints and Photographs Division Washington, D.C.; Accession Number HABS MD,19-HOLWO.V,3C-1

[19] (War of 1812 Claimant, St. Mary's County, Maryland, 1828. Biography: John R. Plater (b. 1767 - d. 1832) 2012). Note: the name is pronounced with a long "a."

[20] (War of 1812 Refugee, St. Mary's County, Maryland, 1814. Biography: Lewis Munroe 2012).

Claim of John Rousby Plater, St. Mary's County, Case #310, Case Files Ca. 1814-28, 3.5 ft. entry 190, Record Group 76, National Archives, College Park. Transcription currently online at: https://msa.maryland.gov/megafile/msa/speccol/sc5300/sc5339/000243/000000/000002/restricted/msa_sc5339_243_2-0017.pdf (accessed 3/21/2023).

[21] (Census of refugee households settled at the North West Arm of Halifax harbor November 2, 1815). The first record shows Lewis Munroe accompanied by one woman and five children. A second record from 1816 shows the Munroe family still there, but with two women and five children, cited currently online, at: novascotia.ca/archives/african-heritage/archives.asp?ID=620&Page=201112574&Transcript=3 (accessed 3/21/2023).

Cogswell's letter (December 24, 1815) to Governor John Sherbrooke referencing the poor condition of the Black Refugees on his lands is attributed to the aforementioned "Census of refugee households settled at the North West Arm of Halifax harbor," in this secondary source: (War of 1812 Refugee, St. Mary's County, Maryland, 1814. Biography: Lewis Munroe 2012).

Information with details about the two other formerly enslaved workers taken from Plater, including further information about their trip to Nova Scotia:

"War of 1812 Refugee, St. Mary's County, Maryland, 1814. Biography: Benjamin Seale." *Archives of Maryland (Biographical Series)*, currently online at: msa.maryland.gov/megafile/msa/speccol/sc5400/sc5496/050900/050984/html/50984bio.html (accessed 3/21/2023).

"War of 1812 Refugee, St. Mary's County, Maryland, 1814. Biography: Stephen Coursey." *Archives of Maryland (Biographical Series)*, currently online at: msa.maryland.gov/megafile/msa/speccol/sc5400/sc5496/051000/051080/html/51080bio.html (accessed 3/21/2023).

[22] Louis Monroe (father of George Monroe who is the subject of this book), gave his age as 33 in the 1850 U.S. Census, putting his birth-year at 1817, but the 1870 and 1880 censuses have Louis possibly understating his age by nine years, logging his birth year as 1820.

[23] There is evidence that at least part of the Munroe family remained in Nova Scotia. Among them was a Lewis Munroe, but the birth years given for him don't match those given by Plater

for either Lewis Sr. (1788) or Lewis Jr. (1811). The 1871 Census of Canada lists a Munroe family, all identified in the record as "African:" Lewis (b. 1832), Catherine (b. 1826), Alice (b. 1864). But the 1881 Census varies significantly: Lewis (b. 1840), Catherine (b. 1801), Alice (b. 1865); also, Catherine and Alice are not listed among the Munroes in Plater's inventory of enslaved people. The data suggest that the Lewis Munroe in the Canadian census listings is not one of the two taken from Sotterley Plantation, but was instead perhaps a nephew. Researchers should also be aware that yet another Lewis Monroe lived some 150 miles east of Halifax, in Canso, N.S., who was born in 1807 in Scotland and whose wife, Elizabeth, was English (1881 Census of Canada).

[24] In 1887 Louis and Mary confirmed in a Superior Court that they'd been "married for more than 40 years" (Mary A. Monroe, Plaintiff vs. Wm. G. Grove and D. P. Allen, Defendants 1887).

Eight out of ten official sources give 1847 as George Monroe's birth-year. Below are the entries for George's recorded age and inferred birth-years per year of recordation:

1850 Census:	Age 7 = 1843
1860 Census:	No Monroe data available
1870 Census:	Age 23 = 1847
1872 Voter Reg:	Age 25 = 1847
1873 Voter Reg:	Age 26 = 1847
1875 Voter Reg:	Age 28 = 1847
1876 Voter Reg:	Age 29 = 1847
1879 Voter Reg:	Age 32 = 1847
1880 Census:	Age 35 = 1845
1884 Voter Reg:	Age 37 = 1847
1886 Voter Reg:	Age 39 = 1847

The most problematic of these is the 1850 Census giving his age as 7 with a birth-year of 1843. This entry carries some weight as it is closest to the event of George's birth, but is quite different from the next census entry from 20 years later and from subsequent entries. It could have been an error of inattention or indifference—one of George's parents may have said "1847" and the census taker only heard the "7," or perhaps there was some reason not yet understood for the Monroes to overstate George's age. A second variance occurs in the 1880 census, but the consistency of the majority of dates, probably furnished by George Monroe himself, indicate his birth-year as 1847.

The voting records researched for this book are from compilations found in 1866-1898 *Great Register, Mariposa County*. It should be noted that voter registrations in the Mariposa Great Register attributed by online indices to the year 1872 often, with closer scrutiny, turn out to be from other years. In order to confirm the correct year, one must look for the registrar's dated signature at the end of each section.

A source typically used in more current articles about George Monroe is his obituary in the *Mariposa Gazette* (November 27, 1886, pg. 3-4, col. 3). In it, the *Gazette* states that in 1855 George was "about 11 years of age," leading to an otherwise unsubstantiated conclusion of 1844 for Monroe's birthyear.

The suggestion of a location for the Monroes' marriage and George Monroe's birthplace is in George Millen's 1897 testimony: "I lived in the same town [as Mary] until later years, she moved out to Columbus, Georgia, from Augusta, Georgia." This sentence, and the fact that he uses the singular "she" rather than, for example, "we" or "they," is so far the only and best evidence that Mary moved to Columbus before her marriage and the birth

204

of her son. By 1850, the U.S. Census Bureau (1850) firmly places Louis, Mary and George Monroe in Columbus, along with Polly Millen who is listed as "Mulatto" and aged 50.

George Monroe's middle name of Frazier is established in his voter registration record of 1872.

[25] U.S. Census Bureau (1850). James Millen also shows up living in Campbell, GA, in the 1880 census. James gives his parents' birthplaces as Georgia and South Carolina, contrary to Mary Millen's (Monroe's) records that indicate that her parents were born in Pennsylvania, suggesting that James may have been Mary's cousin rather than a brother.

According to Frederick Law Olmstead, in 1853 Columbus was the largest manufacturing city south of Richmond, Virginia; see the New Georgia Encyclopedia currently at: georgiaencyclopedia.org/articles/counties-cities-neighborhoods/Columbus (accessed 3/21/2023).

[26] (Black Entrepreneurs in Antebellum America n.d.).

U.S. Census Bureau (1850) lists Lewis Monroe's trade as Barber.

For a glimpse into the life of William Johnson, see (currently available courtesy the National Humanities Center): nationalhumanitiescenter.org/pds/maai/identity/text4/williamjohnsondiary.pdf (accessed 3/21/2023).

[27] (Grant 1885-1886). (May 1987) pp. 473 – 475.

It has been estimated that before the American Civil War, three-to-five thousand people escaped slavery to Mexico, many of whom joined the Mexican military (Baumgartner 2020).

[28] (Zelinsky 1950) pp. 386-401.

[29] (Grant 1885-1886) chapter VI, p. 117.

[30] The 1852 census confirms Louis Monroe's presence in Calaveras County (under Leuis Munroe, Calaveras, California; citing p. 143, State Archives, Sacramento; FHL microfilm 909,229). Also, a passenger list dated April 1, 1852, includes a Louis Monroe arriving in San Francisco via Panama on the steamship Fremont. George Millen does not appear on the list, but listed close to Monroe's name is "J.M. Milliken" which may be a mis-hearing of George Millen See: Louis J. Rasmussen, *San Francisco Ship Passenger Lists. Vol. III: November 7, 1851 to June 17, 1852* (2003; accessed 2/18/2020 on ancestry.com)

Image: [Auburn Ravine, 1852]. Creator/Contributor: Starkweather, Joseph B., photographer (attributed to) (photographer). Date: [1852]. Identifier: DAG-0103; Collection: Cased photographs selected from the collections of the California History Section of the California State Library.

[31] (Coroner, City of San Diego 1897)

[32] (Cobb 1851).

Millen's story about his nephew attending school in Washington, D. C. is corroborated in: *Mariposa Gazette*, November 27, 1886, pg. 3-4, col. 3.

[33] An essay titled "Slaveholding in Antebellum Augusta and Richmond County, Georgia" can currently be found here: latinamericanstudies.org/slavery/Phylon-1987.pdf (accessed 3/21/2023).

[34] Regarding education for African American children, see: (Special Report of the Commissioner of Education on the Condition and Improvement of Public Schools in the District of Columbia: Submitted to the Senate June, L868, and to the House, with Additions, June 13, 1870 1871).

Statistics from the 1850 and 1860 census for U.S. school attendance are broken down into two useful tables in: (Finkleman 2006, April 6).

[35] Ron Chernow, *Grant* (Penguin, 2018), chpt. 5

[36] The Millen quote: "Her husband was so excited, when he heard she was here, he got up and left the county he was in" requires some deconstruction, because (in this single case) I have reinterpreted the transcript. The original text of Millen's statement, probably taken in shorthand during the inquest and later transcribed, reads thus: "Her husband was so excited, when she heard he was here, she got up and left the county he was in." It is impossible (at least for the author) to make sense of this within the larger context of Millen's statement, especially with Millen's next statement that "He left, and she followed him …." In other words, why would she leave the county when she heard Louis was there, after traveling so far to find him, and then follow him? On the other hand, if Millen had delivered the statement in a quick, animated fashion, the clerk may have confused "he" with "she." The error would have been made during the testimony,

and not during the transcription from shorthand to text, as the shorthand symbols for "he" and "she" are easily distinguished.

[37] General census statistics and the estimate of 4,000 African Americans joining the Gold Rush can be found here: blackpast.org/timelines/african-american-history-timeline-1800-1900 (accessed July 26, 2020).

[38] At times, postal carriers stopped at Charleston and Savannah on the way to Panama. See currently online: panamarailroad.org/mail.html (accessed 3/21/2023).

Mileage and average travel-time from New York to San Francisco via Nicaragua was reported in Journal of the Society of Arts, and of the Institutions in Union, Volume 5, January 23, 1857 (London: George Bell 1857), pg. 143. Currently online at: books.google.com/books?id=PDA6AQAAMAAJ&lpg=PA143&ots =jVjP5j5Xqd&dq=Journal%20of%20the%20Society%20of%20Arts %2C%20and%20of%20the%20Institutions%20in%20Union%2C%2 0Volume%205%2C%20January%2023%2C%201857&pg=PA143#v =onepage&q&f=false (accessed 3/21/2023).

The cost for steerage passengers was reported in *Daily Alta California*, March 15, 1853, pg. 3, col. 4. Current dollar-estimates are available on various online calculators such as in2013dollars.com. One article gives the rate for a Butterfield stagecoach trip as $200: truewestmagazine.com/train-and-stagecoach-ticket-prices (accessed 3/21/2023).

There are plenty of accounts to be found about Gold Rush travel routes; here's one currently online: americacomesalive.com/2013/03/06/traveling-west-in-1854-the-story-of-an-11-year-old-girl-and-her-family (accessed 3/21/2023).

³⁹ 1866 Ticket, San Francisco to New York via Nicaragua: This was an alternative to the Panama route. Incidental to the story, the agent named on the ticket—I. W. Raymond—was instrumental in bringing about the Yosemite Grant in 1864, which in turn led to the creation of the National Park System. Also incidentally, the steamer for which the ticket was issued—the *SS America*—is the ship that writer Mark Twain took from San Francisco on his way to New York, just prior to publishing his *"The Celebrated Jumping Frog of Calaveras County"* see currently maritimeheritage.org/vips/marktwain.html (accessed 3/21/2023), and *Daily Alta California*, December 15, 1866, San Francisco. Even more incidentally, it was an earlier version of *SS America* that likely carried Galen Clark from New York on his way to California; see (Lowe and Carpenter 2017) endnote 1, p. 96, cites *NY Daily Times* 10/21/1853 c.5/p.8 (v. 3 no 653).

SS America information currently online at: maritimeheritage.org/ships/steamships.htm#SSAmerica (accessed 3/21/2023).

⁴⁰ (Grant 1885-1886) chapter XIV, also found online at sfmuseum.net/hist9/usgrant.html (accessed 3/21/2023).

⁴¹ For a bit of history of the Panama Railroad currently online: jstor.org/stable/43517551?read-now=1&seq=1#page_scan_tab_contents (accessed 3/21/2023).

⁴² George Monroe obituary: *Mariposa Gazette*, November 27, 1886, pg. 3, col. 4, and *Mariposa Gazette*, November 27, 1886, pg. 3-4, col. 3.

George Millen estimated that Mary headed to Mariposa in early 1854 (in his 1897 Coroner's Inquest testimony). George Monroe's obituary had him arriving in Mariposa one year after his mother, but put Mary's arrival in Mariposa at 1855, a year later than George Millen's estimate.

[43] Millen's location in Weaverville is recorded by the U.S. Census Bureau (1860). Trinity County, California, about 200 miles north of Calaveras County, at the time was a robust gold mining area. Weaverville is located within Trinity Co.

[44] *Mariposa Gazette*, May 31, 1890, pg. 3, col. 6; Louis Monroe's obituary states that he resided "in town."

[45] *Mariposa Gazette*, November 27, 1886, pg. 3-4, col. 3.

[46] Horse-breaking versus training, see: montyroberts.com/starting-not-breaking-a-horse (accessed 3/21/2023).

According to Oxford Languages, the word "livery" comes from Middle English, which adopted the Old French liveree (medieval Latin for 'hand over'), and came over time to refer to the providing of food, clothing, provender for horses, and, eventually, the business of care, stabling, and the renting out of horses and carriages.

[47] Thomas Hill sketch: *San Francisco Chronicle*, June 2, 1895 pg. 1 col. 4. Stereo photograph No. 1159 by Carleton Watkins, online at carletonwatkins.org/getviewbyid.php?id=1001379 (accessed 3/15/2023)

⁴⁸ "Yo Semite or Yo Hamite?" *Mariposa Gazette*, August 8, 1856, pg. 2, col. 3 [Editorial note: "Indigenous" replaces the pejorative "digger," commonly used at the time]. A well-sourced history of the name-origin of Yosemite (Daniel E. Anderson, *Origin of the Word Yosemite*) can currently be found here: yosemite.ca.us/library/origin_of_word_yosemite.html (accessed 3/21/2023).

⁴⁹ James H. Lawrence, *San Francisco Chronicle*, June 2, 1895 pg. 1 col. 4. Historians commonly infer that Clark's first cabin had instead been built near a spring about 700 yards (about 640 meters) to the west of the current Wawona Hotel. This story derives from (Sargent, Galen Clark - Yosemite Guardian 1964) p. 57 [the later Flying Spur Press edition omits source citations]:

> "Contrary to accepted and published belief, Galen's first camp was not on the present site of the Wawona Hotel but clear across the meadow by a spring."

Sargent cites her source as her Aug. 1963 interview with Will Sell Jr., who said he was shown the spring site by Clark. Sargent also writes that the location was corroborated by Sell's contemporary, Clarence Washburn (in both cases, 49 years after Clark's death).

It is important that, in this instance, Sargent used the word "camp" and did not refer to the presence of a structure. Notably Sargent attaches a primary-source to the above quotation citing the *San Francisco Chronicle*, June 2, 1895, which contradicts the notion that Clark's first *cabin* was instead at the spring site.

Sargent's source-attribution also stands out as a rare occurrence — her published books on Yosemite history seldom furnish source citations. A possible explanation for the contradictory footnote is that Sargent, not wishing to overtly dispute a version of the story asserted by her then still-living interviewees, purposely left a tacit clue for future historians to uncover. Or, perhaps she wished to leave an example of the "accepted and published belief," leaving it to the reader to decide which source was more compelling.

A photograph (in the Yosemite Museum and Archives) of Clark at the spring site, giving the date of his planting of four sequoia trees there as 1863, suggests that he may have built a cabin on the site around that year, perhaps to get some privacy away from his hostelry. Also, the drawing of the cabin by famed artist Thomas Hill accompanying the 1895 *Chronicle* article suggests the shape of Wawona Dome looming behind, as the article states, "from a description given by Clark." It is probable that the dome would not have been visible from the closely-forested spring site. Additionally, the picture's caption implies that Clark was directly involved with the *Chronicle* article, which was likely the product of a personal interview with the writer of the article, J. H. Lawrence, lending credence to the story.

[50] *Mariposa Gazette*, June 26, 1857, pg. 2, col. 2.

[51] *Mariposa Gazette*, December 10, 1858, pg. 2, col. 3.

[52] Lemuel Albert Holmes born Dec. 29, 1824 in Pomfret, Connecticut, died Sep. 8, 1862 in Stockton, California. See *The Descendants of George Holmes of Roxbury: 1594-1908* by George Arthur Gray (Press of D. Clapp & son, 1908) p.182, currently online at: books.google.com/books/about/The_Descendants_of_George_Hol mes_of_Roxb.html?id=9-VUAAAAMAAJ (accessed 3/21/2023).

[53] *Mariposa Gazette*, January 1, 1861, pg. 1, col. 4. According to Webster's, the word "tonsorial" derives from the Latin verb tondēre, meaning "to shear, clip or crop."

By the February 12 edition of the *Gazette*, Monroe's ad gives his location as "in the same old place, between the Pine Tree House and the Arcade Saloon" (*Mariposa Gazette*, February 12, 1861, pg. 2, col. 4). The curious spelling of "shampooing" shows up in other ads, as in the *Mariposa Democrat* (1857), so appears to be deliberate.

The fire took place on June 4, 1858. It was reported that 100 structures burned in an hour and a half, fifty-five of which were businesses, according to *Sacramento Daily Union*, June 14, 1858, pg. 1, col. 6.

[54] U.S. Census Bureau (1850).

[55] *Mariposa Gazette*, July 30, 1861, pg. 5. William Crocker was a German immigrant (1860 census) who later taught music in San Francisco (1870 and 1880 census). An advertisement (*Mariposa Democrat* 6/11/1857) for his *Pacific Billiard Saloon* in nearby Hornitos trumpeted: "The Bar is always replete with the best of Wines, Liquors, Cigars, etc. Cold and Warm Baths. Lodging by the night, week or month. A musical entertainment will be given every evening, under the direction of the celebrated pianist CROCKER, assisted by other artists."

[56] *Mariposa Gazette*, December 17, 1861, pg. 1, col. 1-5, pg. 2, col. 1.

[57] (Chernow 2018) chapter 11.

[58] *Mariposa Gazette*, March 18, 1862, pg. 2, col. 1. Quartz Gulch was by Mariposa Creek, just south of Mariposa, and featured the first steam-powered quartz-mill brought in by James Duff in 1849 (*Mariposa Gazette*, January 17, 1873, pg. 2, col. 2). The ruins of the mill were mentioned in connection with the place-name "Quartz Gulch" (Chamberlain 1936), introduction, pg. x. The location is shown as "Fremont's first Mill" in "Quartz Mill Gulch" on the southern perimeter of Mariposa, in an 1861 map: "Las Mariposas Estate Mariposas County California" (1861, Pub. New York, Sarony, Major & Knapp); David Rumsey Historical Map Collection: davidrumsey.com/luna/servlet/detail/RUMSEY~8~1~1821~180008: Las-Mariposas-Estate-Mariposas-Coun (accessed 3/21/2023).

The snow-depth that winter was reported by Galen Clark in *Mariposa Gazette*, December 17, 1861, pg. 2, col. 1.

[59] A couple of sites for calculating current monetary values: in2013dollars.com; westegg.com/inflation (accessed 3/21/2023).

[60] Monroe's 1863 homestead claim of September 10, 1863 was revealed in testimony during the 1888 court case (Mary A. Monroe, Plaintiff vs. Wm. G. Grove and D. P. Allen, Defendants 1887).

[61] (Chernow 2018) p. 858.

[62] *The Elevator*, July 14, 1865 and March 28, 1874 (the latter evidencing Monroe's continued association with the paper). Monroe's letter to the paper appears in *The Elevator*, August 25, 1865, pg. 2, col. 4.

[63] *Mariposa Gazette*, September 16, 1865, pg. 2, col. 3. Also reported in *The Elevator*, October 13, 1865, pg. 3, col. 4.

Moses Rodgers was a successful mining engineer in Gold Rush California. He built a home for his family in 1890 in Stockton, California, which is now on the National Register of Historic Places. Information currently online at: noehill.com/sanjoaquin/nat1978000763.asp (accessed 3/21/2023).

[64] Two current online resources for California's secession movement: parks.ca.gov/?page_id=26775; militarymuseum.org/HistoryCW.html (accessed 3/21/2023).

[65] In his 1936 book *The Call of Gold*, p. 143, Newell D. Chamberlain writes:

> "Many Southerners came out early to the mines with their slaves. Colonel Thorn, one of the founders of Quartzburgh, brought several but freed his 'niggahs,' immediately upon learning that California had been admitted into the Union as a free State. Others waited until President Lincoln's proclamation. The freed slaves generally stayed in close proximity to their former masters and so, after the Civil War, there were fifteen or twenty negro families, living near the southern limits of Hornitos. Prominent among them, was Mose Rodgers, who, for many years was superintendent of the famous Washington mine."

It is ambiguous whether Chamberlain groups Rodgers with Thorn's enslaved workers, or merely refers to him in connection with the other families. Chamberlain's story that Thorn freed the people he'd enslaved is contradicted by the story of a man who remained enslaved by Thorn named Peter Green, recounted later in this book. (Chamberlain 1936) currently available online at: yosemite.ca.us/library/call_of_gold (accessed 3/21/2023).

Regarding Thorn's title, "Colonel" was commonly used as an honorary title, particularly in the southern United States, not necessarily denoting military rank.

In Moses Rodgers' obituary, the *Gazette* writes "Rodgers was born a slave in the State of Kentucky, April 27th, 1845. His real name was Moses Logan, the name Rodgers being adopted in honor of his master, whose name was Rodgers." On the same page, Rodgers' death notice reads "RODGERS- In Stockton, October 20th, 1900, Moses L. Rodgers, a native of Missouri, aged 64 years" *Mariposa Gazette*, October 27, 1900, pg. 1, col. 4 and 7. According to the *San Joaquin County California Death Index*, Rodgers died October 23, 1900, age 64 years, 6 months, 8 days, born in Missouri. This would make his birth date April 15, 1836. Interestingly, in 1900 the U. S. Census recorded Rodgers' information twice, first on June 2 in Stockton as "Mose Rogers," giving his mother's birthplace as Missouri and his father's as "unknown," then, secondly, in Hornitos on June 26, recording his mother's birthplace as Kentucky, and his father's as Virginia.

[66] The Keechi Creek demographic data come from "A History of Leon County" Published by the Leon County News, May 28 1936, contributed to *Genealogy Trails* by Friends For Free Genealogy: genealogytrails.com/tex/pineywoods/leon/history1.html (accessed 3/21/2023).

Account of Thorn's trip to California: (Daughters of Republic of Texas - Volume 1 1995) p. 274.

67 Thorn's stayover in Los Angeles is documented in: *Mariposa Gazette*, November 13, 1897, obituary for Thorn's wife, Mary F. Hardwick.

68 (An Illustrated History of Los Angeles County, California 1889) p.358-359.

69 "Old Records Show Slavery in State," *Madera Tribune*, Volume XXV, Number 108, September 4, 1916, currently online at: https://cdnc.ucr.edu/?a=d&d=MT19160904.2.22&e=-------en--20--1--txt-txIN--------1 (accessed 3/21/2023). The contract releasing Green from Thorn's ownership was dated February 5, 1853.

For history on the "Chivalry Democrats" and the California Fugitive Slave Act: (Smith 2011) pp. 28-63.

70 Charles Davis to Daughter, January 5 [1852], and January 6, 1854, Davis Letters: (Johnson, Domestic Life in the Diggings—The Southern Mines in the California Gold Rush 1999) pp. 116-117; see also (Johnson, Roaring Camp: The Social World of the California Gold Rush 2000) and (Collins 1949), the edited writings of Samuel Ward, brother of Julia Ward Howe, describing what he called "Thorn Villa" and the surrounding area during his time there in 1851.

Note: "Black" substituted by the author for the pejorative "darkey" in the original text.

71 *Mariposa Democrat* (Hornitos, CA), June 11, 1857 pg. 2, col. 2.

72 *Mariposa Democrat* (Hornitos, CA), December 31, 1857 pg. 1, col. 2, and pg. 2, col. 3.

[73] (Woodson and Logan, The Journal of Negro History 1918) p. 48. Green was freed on August 7, 1855.

[74] Information on the Washington Mine is from: "California Journal of Mines and Geology," Vol 53, Nos. 1 & 2 (State of California Department of Natural Resources, Division of Mines, Ferry Building, San Francisco, July 25, 1957), p. 178, currently available online at: archive.org/details/californiajourna53cali/page/178 (accessed July 26, 2020).

Chamberlain's quote: (Chamberlain 1936).

[75] A brief discussion on Reconstruction with historian Henry Louis Gates, Jr. can currently be found here (Courtesy National Public Radio, *Fresh Air*, interview with Terry Gross, April 3, 2019, 2:19 PM ET,): npr.org/templates/transcript/transcript.php?storyId=709094399 (accessed 3/21/2023).

[76] Photograph courtesy Mariposa Museum and History Center. Caption: (Chamberlain 1936).

[77] The Center for Great Plains Studies project, spearheaded by Richard Edwards, promises to uncover much more of the history of this subject (Black Homesteaders in the Great Plains 2018).

See also: washingtonpost.com/opinions/the-disappearing-story-of-the-black-homesteaders-who-pioneered-the-west/2018/07/05/ca0b51b6-7f09-11e8-b0ef-fffcabeff946_story.html?noredirect=on&utm_term=.838488f5658c (*Washington Post* July 5, 2018) (accessed 3/21/2023).

[78] In Sacramento from October 25th–29th, Moses L. Rodgers represented Mariposa at the last of four so-called "Colored Conventions" (Proceedings of the California State Convention of Colored Citizens 1865) p. 4. The quoted resolutions of the *"Report of the Committee on Industrial Pursuits"* are on page 20 of the same document.

[79] *The Elevator*, December 8, 1865, pg. 2, col. 5. Also reported are various appointees: "Executive Committee of Mariposa: James Duff, W. A. Davis, G. Ward, Lewis A. Monroe, A. P. Matthews of Mariposa, J. J. Levy of Hornitos, J. Gilley of Coulterville." The "E. Quivers" mentioned refers to Emmanuel Quivers, whose daughter, Sara Jane Quivers, married Moses Rodgers in 1873.

[80] (Proceedings of the California State Convention of Colored Citizens 1865) p. 14). Rodgers also reported on behalf of Merced County: "Male Adults–11; Female Adults–8; Children–8."

[81] (Chernow 2018) chapter 25

[82] *Mariposa Free Press*, April 1, 1866.

[83] *Mariposa Gazette*, December 15, 1866, pg. 3, col. 1.

[84] (Plante 2001).

[85] The full typewritten caption accompanying the same image in a photograph album belonging to Estella Washburn (1864-1950) reads "Photo was made between 1852 and 1862. Believed to be about 1862. The four men lived in the cabin at left side of picture. They are L to R : Henry Washburn, Chas. or Herman Schlageter, John Washburn & Jim Barrett." The image was published by Charles Bierstadt, who is known to have photographed in

Mariposa in 1870, three years after the construction of the Schlageter Hotel which appears in the picture. Thus, the dates in the caption appear to be incorrect, raising some doubt about the identification of the figures. Henry Washburn did indeed live in Mariposa in the general time-frame of the photograph, but also at that time, all of his brothers lived in Vermont. Whether one or more of them came to Mariposa for a visit remains unknown.

[86] Terry's losses were reported in: *Mariposa Free Press*, April 1, 1866. Relocation of Terry's stables: *Mariposa Gazette*, September 22, 1866, pg. 2, col. 5. An advertisement dates Terry's stable to September, 1860: *Mariposa Gazette*, July 16, 1861, pg. 4, col. 4 (ad dated Sept. 17).

"Colonel" was commonly used in the southern United States as an honorary, not necessarily military, title.

[87] *Mariposa Gazette*, January 19, 1867, pg. 2, col. 5.

[88] A.H. Washburn's birth year: "Washburn Genealogy" (1907), transcribed (typewritten) by Clarence Washburn (February 12, 1931), (Wawona Washburn Hartwig Papers, Yosemite Museum and Archives).

[89] Seth, Ed, and Henry Washburn's whereabouts are established here: Transcript of *Letter, Edward Washburn to Martha Washburn*, June 15, 1856; Transcript of *Letter, E. P. Washburn to S. C. Washburn*, 5/13/1859; *Will of Seth Caswell Washburn*; (Wawona Washburn Hartwig Papers, Yosemite Museum and Archives).

Seth Washburn's death is documented in a transcript of the *Bellows Falls Times*, March 9, 1860, Vol. 5, No. 10, p. 2/col.2

(Wawona Washburn Hartwig Papers, Yosemite Museum and Archives).

[90] Washburn/Bruce marriage reported in: *Mariposa Gazette,* December 23, 1865, pg. 2, col. 5.

Reports of the Bruce & Washburn mine came from *Mariposa Free Press,* November 5 and 25, 1865, and April 21, 1866 (research courtesy Tom Phillips).

In 1882 Moses Rodgers would become part-owner of the Eureka Mine (formerly known as the Quartz Mountain Mine), according to: *Annual Report of the Director of the Mint* (1882), p.58.

Washburn and Bruce lease, and output of the Eureka Mine reported in: *Mariposa Gazette,* June 2, 1866, p. 1/col. 1.

[91] *New York Times* October 29, 1865.

[92] *Mariposa Gazette,* January 19, 1867, pg. 2, col. 7.

[93] *Mariposa Gazette,* February 2, 1867, pg. 4, col. 2. McCready's new "Yo Semite Stables" ad appears on the same page. Previous ads for McCready's read "NEW LIVERY STABLE" from his original opening ad in 1861 up to and including *Mariposa Gazette,* January 19, 1867.

[94] (Ad dated 3/16/1867) *Mariposa Gazette,* April 6, 1867, pg. 4, col. 2.

[95] *Mariposa Gazette,* March 20, 1868, pg. 2, col. 7 (this ad, appearing in the March 20, 1868 issue, is tagged at the bottom, "March 13,

1867," which appears to be a typo; the correct date is probably March 13, 1868).

[96] *Mariposa Gazette*, November 27, 1886, pg. 3-4, col. 3.

[97] *Mariposa Mail*, June 22, 1867, pg. 3, col. 1. Washburn reportedly told Ben C. Truman of having employed fifty stage drivers during peak years.

The name "Parteta" shows up again in *Mariposa Gazette*, July 3, 1875, pg. 3, col. 1-2 as "Ceneral Partida," possibly a typographical error meant to be "General" Partida. U.S. Census Bureau (1870) lists Stephen Partida, a laborer living in Mariposa and born in Mexico c. 1810. The 1880 census spells his name Estevan Partida, and occupation as "porter."

[98] Washburn's partnering with McCready and the consolidation of their stables and stock was announced in *Mariposa Mail*, April 9, 1869, pg. 3, col. 1, and in an advertisement dated 4/23/1869 in *Mariposa Gazette*, June 18, 1869, pg. 4, col. 4. John R. McCready established a livery stable in 1861 (*Mariposa Gazette*, January 29, 1861, pg. 3, col. 7), and was guiding saddle trains into Yosemite by 1865 (*Mariposa Gazette*, July 8, 1865, pg. 2, col. 4).

"Saddle-train" is a descriptive term for the method still used for guiding travelers, often single-file, on horseback.

As seen in the ad from 1868, Washburn's "Mammoth Tree Livery Stable" at 7th & Bullion appears to have been extended to Main St. (now State Highway 49). On March 28, 1869 Washburn deeded to McCready a parcel of land on the north-west corner of Charles St. & 6th called the "Upper Stable," and McCready deeded to Washburn a parcel on the south-east corner of Charles St. & 4th called "Washburn & McCready's Lower Stable." The reason for the land swap is not recorded. Copies of the deeds are in the Yosemite Museum & Archives.

[99] The 14th Amendment to the United States Constitution; currently online at: loc.gov/rr//program/bib/ourdocs/14thamendment.html (accessed 3/21/2023).

[100] May 22, 1868, pg. 2, col. 4. Incidentally, Louis Monroe reported the following accident, recounted in *The Elevator*, June 18, 1869, pg. 2, col. 1:

> "Accident at Mariposa.—We learn, by a letter received from Mr. L. A. Monroe, that a distressing occurrence happened at Mariposa, on 10th instant, which caused the death of Mr. Sandy Jackson. He was sinking a well, and while down he was taken suddenly sick. He cried to those above, and while they were raising him up he fell out of the bucket. He was got out immediately, but expired soon after. Mr. Jackson was born in Loudon County, Virginia, and was about 52 years old. He leaves a wife and one child."

Louis Monroe remained on the list of "Agents for the Elevator" until at least 1869: *The Elevator*, February 26, 1869, pg. 1, col. 1.

[101] *Mariposa Gazette*, June 17, 1870, pg. 3, col. 1.

[102] *Mariposa Gazette*, May 26, 1871, pg. 3, col. 1. Sources suggests that the stage may have been constructed by the firm of Milton Henderson and E. G. Clark; see carriagemuseum.org/articles/m-p-henderson-son/ (accessed 3/21/2023). Two examples of stages attributed to Henderson are in the collection of the Yosemite

Museum & Archives, and often on display at the Yosemite History Center in Wawona, Yosemite National Park.

[103] *Mariposa Mail*, July 3, 1868, pg. 2, col. 4. Regarding the Mariposa Mail, according to a transcribed obituary from the *Mariposa Gazette*, Nov. 24, 1888: "[Angevine Reynolds was] elected County Clerk ... While still in the Clerk's office he established the *Mariposa Mail* in 1868 and continued to publish it till 1871. In 1874, he bought the *Mariposa Gazette*, which he has owned and, either separately or in partnership, published ever since." Cited at mariposacounty.sfgenealogy.org/ObitsP-R.html (accessed 11/7/23).

[104] *Mariposa Gazette*, June 21, 1879, pg. 3, col. 2-3.

[105] *Mariposa Gazette*, June 14, 1879, pg. 3, col. 2.

[106] *Mariposa Gazette*, May 12, 1871, pg. 2, col. 3: regarding competition with Washburn & McCready, " ... the tourist can now leave Modesto (temporary terminus of the San Joaquin Valley Branch Central Pacific line) ... taking Fisher & Co.'s stages ...." through Mariposa and part way to Clark & Moore's.

Mariposa Gazette, May 27, 1870, pg. 2, col. 1, includes several advertisements and articles report on connecting Yosemite travel with the transcontinental railroad.

Public notice showing the Fishers and others (conspicuously absent are Washburn and McCready) organizing a company to complete a stage road from Mariposa to Clark & Moore's, the Mariposa Grove, and Yosemite Valley appeared in: *Mariposa Gazette*, February 4, 1870, pg. 2, col. 1 & 7. The section of road from White & Hatch's hotel (about 12 miles east of Mariposa) via

Cold Spring to Clark & Moore's was completed by this group, opened by July, 1870.

Though roadbuilder John Conway is often credited for engineering this road, no primary sources corroborate this notion, and his name is not mentioned among the 12 members of the road building company, the complete list of names as follows: "J. H. Budd, Sam'l Fisher, C. C. Pendegast, Zenas Fisher, F. Bonafana, F. S. Bolden, J. R. Campbell, Charles Bowan, J. W. Wilcox, Alex Dearing, Galen Clark, Edwin Moore."

A later article in the *Gazette*, quoted later in these end-notes, confirms that while John Conway did not engineer the first stage road to Clark & Moore's, he did engineer a significant replacement section of the road in 1886: see *Mariposa Gazette*, February 6, 1886, pg. 3, col. 1.

[107] *Mariposa Gazette*, May 27, 1870, pg. 2, col. 7; article on pg. 2, col. 2. Within three months, Gordon & Ridgway would add the Coulterville route to their offerings (*Mariposa Gazette*, August 12, 1870).

[108] Peter Gordon working for Washburn (*Mariposa Gazette*, June 12, 1875, pg. 2, col. 4). Peter Gordon's son Tom Gordon was referred to as Washburn's "chief reinsman" (*Mariposa Gazette*, February 10, 1877, pg. 3, col. 1). Tom's son Eddie Gordon was driving stage for the same company in 1912 per a letter from Clarence Washburn 9/21/1912 (Wawona Washburn Hartwig Papers, Yosemite Museum and Archives). Eddie's son Albert Gordon was hired by Clarence Washburn (Henry's nephew) in 1933 to run the Wawona Hotel boiler-house (Gordon and Reynolds 1994) p. 81.

Fisher's cooperation with Washburn appears in this advertisement, " … by Central Pacific Railroad to Merced, thence by Fisher & Co.'s stage line to Mariposa, connecting with Washburn & McCready's line of stages and carriages which run regularly between Mariposa & Clark & Moore's:" *Mariposa Gazette*, May 17, 1872, pg. 2, col. 5.

[109] "The first vote" drawn by A.R. Waud. Illus. from: Harper's weekly, v. 11, no. 568 (1867 November 16), p. 721 (title page).

[110] The 15th Amendment to the United States Constitution; currently online at: loc.gov/rr/program/bib/ourdocs/15thamendment.html (accessed 3/21/2023).

[111] *Mariposa Gazette*, April 22, 1870, pg. 2, col. 3.

[112] *Mariposa Gazette*, January 12, 1872, pg. 3, col. 1, so far the only occurrence of Mary Monroe's middle name, Ann.

[113] *Mariposa Gazette*, June 23, 1871, pg. 3, col. 1. U.S. Census Bureau (1870) lists all three of the Monroe family on the same page as J.B. Cook and John Bruce, among others, all inhabiting the same district that included the town of Mariposa. Voter registrations show that Louis took up residence at the ranch by 1873.

[114] *Mariposa Gazette*, August 4, 1871, pg. 2, col. 4. This account, along with a photograph from four years previous, currently stand as the earliest primary sources regarding carriages in Yosemite Valley. Photographic evidence shows the presence of a wheeled vehicle in Yosemite Valley as early as 1867 (see Carleton Watkins, *The Sentinel, 3270 Feet. Hutching's Hotel, Yosemite Valley, Mariposa Co.,* 1867, mammoth-plate albumen print, 20 1/2 by 15

3/4 in.). Currently online at:
carletonwatkins.org/Gallery/igallery_pages.php?page_id=11&m=d
and
sothebys.com/en/auctions/ecatalogue/2007/photographs-n08349/lot.116.html (accessed 3/21/2023).

According to historian Shirley Sargent (Sargent, Galen Clark - Yosemite Guardian 1964) p. 48, Galen Clark packed in and assembled the first carriage in Yosemite Valley in 1870, and James Hutchings repeated the feat in August, 1871. The Hutchings story is confirmed in *Mariposa Gazette*, August 11, 1871, pg. 2, col. 3: "Yesterday J. M. Hutchings' new stage, the 'Pioneer,' was packed down the mountains on mules and made its first trip up the valley …." But regarding the origin of the Clark story, there is only one early source which, rather than providing corroboration, instead throws the Clark story into question: Mrs. H. J. Taylor quotes "Charles Tuttle," oddly omitting his last name, his full name being Charles Tuttle Leidig (b. March 8, 1869, d. December 2, 1956; see California Death Index, 1940-1997, Charles Tuttle Leidig, 02 Dec 1956; Department of Public Health Services, Sacramento).

According to Taylor's book:

"[Clark] brought the first wagon into Yosemite Valley. Charles Tuttle, the first white boy born in Yosemite, rehearsed the sensation created by this event: 'I was a boy of eight or nine years when the first wagon was brought into the Valley. Galen Clark had it packed in on mule back. I had never been out of the Valley and had never seen a wagon. Everybody was interested to see it assembled. When all was in readiness three or four days were given to celebrate the event and everybody living in the Valley had a free ride; I will never forget those days!'" (M. H. Taylor 1936)

This appears to be the problematic origin of the Clark story. If Leidig was "eight or nine years when the first wagon was brought into the Valley," that would put the year as 1877—three years after stage travel had become common in Yosemite. Conversely, if Clark brought the first wagon in 1870, Leidig at one year old would not have remembered the event.

A possible explanation is that in 1871, Washburn and McCready, returning to their business in Mariposa, left their wagon with Clark. The quoted section of Taylor's book is currently online here: yosemite.ca.us/library/yosemite_indians_and_other_sketches/galen_clark.html (accessed 3/21/2023).

[115] *Mariposa Gazette*, October 13, 1871, pg. 3, col. 1.

[116] The *Mariposa Gazette* reference to the purchase of "Boomershine's stage line" is a bit vague. Jonathan Boomershine was a stage-driver for a line owned by Simon Shoup, in Sonora, California. Less than a year before Washburn & McCready's purchase, Shoup had announced "I am not responsible for any debts contracted in my name by J. Boomershine & Ed. Harrison, and I will not pay them." Still, Shoup's advertisements for his Sonora stage business continue, with Ed Harrison as his San Francisco agent, and Shoup was on hand to drive his stage at the opening of the Big Oak Flat Road in July, 1874. A possible explanation could be that Shoup settled his debt by giving part-ownership to Boomershine, who promptly sold his interest to Washburn & McCready, while part of the business continued to operate under Shoup's proprietorship. But the details remain in

question; in a response to a May 27, 1871 news article, a drug-store proprietor in nearby Snelling wrote, "I wish to correct a statement made by your Coulterville correspondent … Baumbershine [*sic*], Harrison & Co., have never owned or run a line between this place and Snelling, nor even to Modesto, where the stage is now running. The line is known as the "Coulterville and Yosemite Stage Line," and Mr. Baumbershine is the driver between this place and Modesto. Yours, &c., N. A. Cody, A'gt." - *Merced County Sun*, June 10, 1871; currently online at: cdnc.ucr.edu/?a=d&d=MCS18710610.2.6&srpos=2&e=-------en--20--1--txt-txIN-Baumershein-------1 (accessed 7/18/2022)

[117] "Paint your wagons:" *Mariposa Gazette*, July 30, 1898, pg. 1, col. 2.

[118] Washburn east coast visits: *Mariposa Gazette*, November 24, 1871, pg. 3, col. 2. Bear Creek to be renamed "Ashmore:" *Mariposa Gazette*, November 17, 1871, pg. 3, col. 1; the attribution for the name was a Colonel Nelson Ashmore, evidently a Southern Pacific Railroad executive as implied by an article in the Mariposa Free Press, referenced in *Grass Valley* [California] *Morning Union*, Volume 9, Number 1275, 14 January 1871. Bear Creek renamed Merced: *Mariposa Gazette*, February 9, 1872, pg. 2, col. 2.

[119] *Mariposa Gazette*, May 17, 1872, pg. 3, col. 1. Washburn's return from the east was reported in: *Mariposa Gazette*, April 5, 1872, pg. 3, col. 1.

[120] *Mariposa Gazette*, June 14, 1871, pg. 2, col. 2.

[121] "California Great Registers, 1866-1910," p. 8, entry #856, Voter Registration, Mariposa, Mariposa, California, United States, county clerk offices, California; FHL microfilm 976,934.

[122] *Mariposa Gazette*, January 31, 1873, pg. 2, col. 5. Other entries in the Mariposa Gazette reveal alternate spellings for the ranch-owners near Monroe's as John Keough (c. 1823 – 1909) and possibly James Mallon.

[123] *Mariposa Gazette*, April 17, 1874, pg. 3, col. 2.

[124] Monroe was hired by Washburn and McCready most likely in 1867, as discussed earlier in the book.

[125] Timing of the Merced-Mariposa stage was reported in: *Mariposa Gazette*, November 8, 1872, pg. 3, col. 1. Regarding the Coulterville route, *Mariposa Gazette*, May 29, 1874, pg. 3, col. 1: "Washburn & McCready have put on a line of stages between Merced and Coulterville …. They have plenty of saddle and pack animals for those portions of the route requiring horse back riding."

Monroe's change of residence to Yosemite is documented in: "California Great Registers, 1866-1910,", and California State Library; Sacramento, California; *Great Registers, 1866-1898*; Collection Number: *4-2A*; CSL Roll Number: *26*; FHL Roll Number: *976937*

[126] "End-men" were so called because of their positions on the right and left sides of the stage.

[127] Photograph by John P. Soule No. 1295, "Clark & Moore's Hotel, on the Mariposa Road, 25 miles from Yo-Semite Valley."

[128] Originally published in Grace Greenwood (pseudonym of Sara Jane Lippincott), "Notes of Travel: Eight Days in the Yosemite" *New York Times* (July 27, 1872), pg. 2 col. 5. [NYT online]; quoted here from: (Greenwood and aka Lippincott 1873) pp. 303–365.

The route taken by the Lippincott party was advertised earlier by Washburn & McCready in *Mariposa Gazette*, May 17, 1872, pg. 3, col. 1.

[129] *Mariposa Gazette*, June 9, 1871, pg. 3, col. 1. The biblical quote is from Isaiah 34:4.

[130] *Mariposa Gazette*, July 3, 1874, pg. 3, col. 1-2, and August 14, 1874, pg. 3, col. 1.

[131] Advertisement for Washburn & McCready "private stage line to Yo Semite via Coulterville and Mariposa:" *Mariposa Gazette*, July 10, 1874, pg. 2, col. 7. On the same page is news that a group had "purchased Fisher & Co.'s stage line, and intend running it as an opposition [to Washburn & McCready] to Yo Semite."

The opening of the Coulterville Road is reported in: *Mariposa Gazette*, June 26, 1874, pg. 3, col. 1. The source for Monroe's having driven the first stage on the Coulterville Road resides in a private collection and has not been made public.

McCready's death on August 12 is reported in: *Mariposa Gazette*, August 14, 1874, pg. 3, col. 1.

[132] The purchase of Clark & Moore's "on Monday last" (Dec. 22): *Mariposa Gazette*, December 26, 1874, pg. 3, col. 2.

"The New Yo Semite Road," *Mariposa Gazette*, December 19, 1874, pg. 3, col. 2; contract called for a road "from Clark & Moore's … to the Hermitage—within four miles of the Valley" to be completed by May 1, 1875. Washburn's two new partners were Emory "Wash" Chapman and William F. Coffman. On January 25, 1875, Chapman & Coffman purchased from the estate of John R. McCready his half-ownership in the firm of Washburn & McCready (referenced in a contract dated March 9, 1877, Wawona Washburn Hartwig Papers, Yosemite Museum and Archives).

[133] "Proceedings of the Board of Supervisors, Nov. 2," *Mariposa Gazette*, November 7, 1874, pg. 2, col. 5. The wording of the *Gazette* article makes it clear that it was the bridge that was in the process of construction and not the road, the layout for which Washburn was still in the process of obtaining a permit).

The reason for emphasizing this rather fine point is that there is an unsourced story that the Wawona Covered Bridge was not newly built, but was instead Clark's 1868 bridge which Washburn later covered (Sargent, Yosemite's Historic Wawona 1979) p. 23. This story is supported by an 1872 photograph (see next endnote) showing internal structural similarity between the two versions of the bridge.

[134] Photograph 1872 by Eadweard Muybridge. This photo appears in *Sun Pictures of the Yo Semite Valley, Cal.* (Coyne & Relyea; Knight & Leonard, Printers, Chicago 1874); caption in the publication reads "Thomas Houseworth & Co., Photos Merced River (At Clark & Moore's.) Yo-Semite Valley No. 82" (image courtesy Dennis Kruska).

[135] *Mariposa Gazette*, January 16, 1875, pg. 3, col. 1:

"We are informed by Road Master Peter McDermott, who has just returned from the South Fork, that the new Road being built from that place to Yo Semite Valley, by Washburn, Chapman & Co., is progressing as well as can be expected. There is at least 110 hands employed upon the work, the rain, except when it is falling will not retard the work."

[136] *Mariposa Gazette*, April 24, 1875, pg. 3, col. 2. The grand opening for the road was covered in: *Mariposa Gazette*, July 24 & 31, 1875, pg. 3, col. 1.

[137] (Lester 1873). James Lamon lived in Yosemite Valley in the 1860s and early 1870s.

John Muir mentions the Hermitage in "In the Yo-semite: Holidays Among the Rocks," *New York Tribune*, January 1, 1872. A description of the stage route from Clark & Moore's to Yosemite Valley mentions the Hermitage: *Mariposa Gazette*, December 19, 1874, pg. 3, col. 2. "Hermitage" also appears on the Wheeler survey map of 1883.

[138] The Monroe Ranch was 3.5 miles south of Mormon Bar, at the bottom of the map, and White & Hatch's (mentioned by Sara Jane Lippincott) was five miles east of Bootjack.

Map credit: Delineated by Ann Kero (2001), NPS Roads & Bridges Recording Program, National Park Service, U. S. Department of the Interior: Historic American Engineering Record, National Park Service, Addendum: Yosemite National Park Roads & Bridges, Yosemite Vicinity, Mariposa & Tuolumne Counties, California; Sheet 3 of 19, Historic American Engineering Record CA-117. This beautifully illustrated map was reformatted to fit in the book. The originals may be found online here: loc.gov/pictures/item/ca1673.sheet.00005a (accessed 3/21/2023).

[139] *Mariposa Gazette*, July 3, 1875, pg. 3, col. 1-2.

[140] Observations regarding the number of horses trained by each driver were shared by Yosemite National Park Service Ranger/Stage-driver Burrel "Buckshot" Maier in Wawona, CA in 2019 (author interview). A description of the breakdown of terms for a six-horse team may be found here: truewestmagazine.com/article/in-a-six-team-stagecoach-you-had-the-leaders-and-the-wheelers (accessed 3/21/2023).

[141] Monroe's move to Merced: California State Library; Sacramento, California; *Great Registers, 1866-1898*; Collection Number: *4-2A*; CSL Roll Number: *26*; FHL Roll Number: *976937*

[142] *Mariposa Gazette*, August 24, 1878, pg. 3, col. 1: Shelly shared a ranch near Sherlock's Creek with two partners.

The date for Shelly's construction of the Long White is inferred from *Mariposa Gazette*, December 7, 1878, pg. 3, col. 3: "He [Shelly] was the architect and builder of the hotel completed at that place [Big Tree Station] about two years since."

Shelly's birth is given as December, 1837 (U.S. Census bureau, 1900); citing enumeration district (ED) 30, sheet 4A, family 107, NARA microfilm publication T623 (Washington, D.C.: National Archives and Records Administration, 1972.); FHL microfilm 1,240,087.

"History of the family of Joseph John and Carolina Shelly 1834-1915" (written by an unnamed child of Joseph Shelly's son,

William). Posted 26 Mar 2019 by Shelly family of Inyo County, California at ancestry.com/mediaui-viewer/collection/1030/tree/117553194/person/402035832419/media/ba978ebf-798e-4f21-b7fa-d1b45c1c93a7?_phsrc=INl2484&usePUBJs=true (copy in author's files) (accessed July 29, 2020). Joseph Shelly died Dec. 15, 1915, in Bishop, California.

[143] *Mariposa Gazette*, May 12, 1877, pg. 3, col. 5.

[144] *Mariposa Gazette*, March 17, 1877, pg. 3, col. 1.

Deed of Sale, March 8, 1877 (Wawona Washburn Hartwig Papers, Yosemite Museum and Archives), shows that Washburn's $20,000 purchase from Chapman & Coffman included their half of the hotel, substantial attached acreage, the bridge over the South Fork of the Merced River, a nearby sawmill, the roads connecting Big Tree Station to Yosemite Valley and Mariposa, and what had been McCready's half-ownership in his partnership with Washburn, but did not mention horses and stages.

The quoted *Gazette* article reporting that Cook and Bruce purchased the interests of Chapman and Coffman is not reflected in the *Deed of Sale*, which gives Washburn as the purchaser. The percentage of the business that was sold, and the amount put up by Cook and Bruce, is not revealed in the *Deed*.

(Reynolds and Phillips 1999) p. 33, gives Bruce as ½ owner of Big Tree Station. Sargent also has Bruce as ½ owner of the hotel, but in regard to the Yosemite Stage & Turnpike Co. (formed in November, 1877), Sargent has Bruce's and Cook's shares as ¼, and Washburn owning ½ (Sargent, *Yosemite's Historic Wawona* 1979) p. 28. Further research will hopefully shine light on these transactions; sources were not provided by either Reynolds or Sargent.

[145] Cook sells his drug store, *Mariposa Gazette*, March 17, 1877, pg. 3, col. 1:

"Our town and county has met with a loss which seems to us almost irreparable; Squire [Charles] Bruce has been a resident of this county upwards of twenty years. He has held positions of honor, and offices of trust in our town and county, for many years in which he has acquitted himself with satisfaction to all within the home circle, and with great credit to himself. For several years past he has had charge of J. J. Cook's drug store, and for the same length of time has held the position of Secretary of the Odd-Fellows Lodge of this place. The drug store having changed hands the Squire has removed to Merced, to assist the new firm of Washburn, Cook and Bruce in their stage and passenger office at that place."

Charles Bruce was John B. Bruce's father; information currently online at: mariposaresearch.net/bruce.html (accessed 3/21/2023).

"Washburn & Bruce Upper Livery Stable" documented in: *Deed of Sale*, March 8, 1877 (Wawona Washburn Hartwig Papers, Yosemite Museum and Archives)

A *Gazette* ad also includes Bruce, "Mammoth Tree and Yo Semite Livery Stable" documented in: *Mariposa Gazette*, March 17, 1877, pg. 2, col. 7 (ad dated Jan. 1, with a typo for the year—"75"—which should read "77").

" … annual meeting of the stockholders of the Yo Semite Stage and Turnpike Company … A. H. Washburn, Sam Miller and J. J. Cook comprise the Board of Directors:" *Mariposa Gazette*, November 10, 1883, pg. 3, col. 1.

[146] Taylor's reference comes from classical Latin *facilis dēscensus Avernī* (Virgil Aeneid 6. 126), "easy is the descent into Hell."

Taylor's quote, "get out of the way, you are all unlucky," is a line from a campaign song c. 1844, popular when Whig party candidate Henry Clay opposed James K. Polk in the U.S. presidential race.

Fanning mills were commonly used on farms for separating grains, such as wheat, from unwanted weed-seeds and dirt, etc.

From Greek mythology, Briareus was a hundred-handed, fifty-headed god of sea-storms.

"Cold Spring" now appears as Cold Springs on maps.

[147] Scanned image courtesy the Douglas and Marilynn Guske collection

[148] (B. F. Taylor 1878) pp. 202-205, 213-214.

[149] The list of celebrities and all subsequent quotes from Ben C. Truman are from his articles: (Truman, Knights of the Lash: Old Time Stage Drivers of the West Coast March 1898), and (Truman, The Passing of a Sierra Knight July 1903). These articles and others by Truman are reprinted in: (Kurutz 2005).

Peculiar to Truman's 1898 article is his use of the name "Alfred" as a sort of nickname for George Monroe — so far, this appellation for Monroe has not been found in any other documents.

Of the names provided by Truman (except for Grant), I have found no additional sources to corroborate whether Monroe carried them; however, at least five are known to have visited Yosemite through Wawona. According to the *Mariposa Gazette* (MG): Sherman (MG 4/22/1882), Dana (MG 4/21/1883), Langtry (MG 7/12/1884), Sullivan (MG 6/20/1885). Rutherford B. Hayes' visit was covered in: *Fresno Weekly Expositor*, December 22, 1880. Garfield's visit (when he was still a member of Congress) is documented in his own diary entries for May 12 – 21, 1875, currently online at: loc.gov/resource/mss21956.mss21956-002_0015_1135/?sp=271 (accessed 3/21/2023).

[150] Monroe's card employs the same stagecoach graphic used on the Yosemite Stage & Turnpike Company letterhead image (c. 1900) reproduced at the beginning of Chapter I (letterhead image courtesy Yosemite Museum and Archives)

[151] *Mariposa Gazette*, December 7, 1878, pg. 3, col. 3. The article gives the date of the fire as "Saturday morning last" which fell on November 30. Sargent gives the date of the fire as November 29, 1878 (unattributed), as well as the Tom Gordon reference (Sargent, Yosemite's Historic Wawona 1979) pp. 32-33.

[152] *Mariposa Gazette*, December 28, 1878, pg. 3, col. 1.

[153] *Mariposa Gazette*, April 5, 1879, pg. 3, col. 1. April 1, 1879 was given by Sargent as the opening date for the new building (Sargent, Yosemite's Historic Wawona 1979) p. 33 (unattributed), but the Gazette shows the "first party" of the season still in

Mariposa on that date, the new building was still under construction, and the Long White would easily accommodate a party of ten with rooms to spare.

[154] Photographs used in the collage: "Clark's near Big Tree Grove on the Mariposa Trail to Yosemite," by Carleton Watkins (1866 Mammoth Plate No. 105; Neaf and Hult-Lewis No. 976), and an 1879 Watkins photograph identified as "Clarks, or Big Tree Station on route to Yosemite Valley" (Lowe and Carpenter 2017) p. 70.

[155] The opening date of the new building inferred from "Index of hotel registers:" Box979.447 Y-16b, Yosemite Museum and Archives. Though listed in the index, the June 5, 1879 hotel register is missing from the Yosemite Museum and Archives).

Shelly still at work: *Mariposa Gazette*, June 28, 1879, pg. 3, col. 1.

Monroe's change of residence to Yosemite is documented in his voter-registration, California State Library; Sacramento, California; *Great Registers, 1866-1898*; Collection Number: *4-2A*; CSL Roll Number: *26*; FHL Roll Number: *976937*

[156] Author's photograph of the Wawona Hotel c. 2000, and photograph titled "Big Tree Station, Mariposa Road and Big Trees," by J. J. Reilly c. 1876 (Lowe and Carpenter 2017) p. 65.

[157] *Mariposa Gazette*, April 5, 1879, pg. 3, col. 1.

[158] *Mariposa Gazette*, April 12, 1879, pg. 3, col. 1.

[159] Information regarding "Cannonball" Green currently online courtesy "Legends of Kansas" at

legendsofkansas.com/cannonballstage.html and courtesy "The Historical Marker Database" at hmdb.org/m.asp?m=65268 (accessed 3/21/2023).

Clarence Washburn Diaries, August 4, 1925: Here Washburn refers to one of the successors of the horse-drawn stages, a Pierce-Arrow auto-stage: "Left Merced came direct to Wawona at noon on Cannonball. Everything ok. Travel good ...." (Washburn Papers, Yosemite Museum and Archives).

[160] "New Road To Yosemite," *Daily Alta California*, May 19, 1879 p.2 col.3
Currently online at: cdnc.ucr.edu/?a=d&d=DAC18790519&e=------en--20-DAC-1--txt-txIN-may+19+1879-------1 (accessed August 3, 2020).

[161] The word "Wawona," with similar-sounding variations, is recorded as denoting the giant sequoia by several local cultural groups:

Talinchi Yokuts (Coarsegold):	wah-ho´-nah.
Monache/Northfork Mono (North Fork)	wah-ho´-nah; waw-wo´-nah.
Monache (Auberry)	wah´-ho-nab´.
Monache-Yokuts/Wobonuch (Mill Flat)	wo´-ho-nab-b.
Yokuts-Monache/Entimbich (Dunlap)	wo-ho-nab´-bah.
Monache/Waksachi (Tulare County)	wo´-hß7-nab´-b´.

(Davis-King 1999), citing (Merriam 1979).

Muir's reference to Wawona: (Wolfe 1979) p. 209. Wolfe offers this comment in the footnote for Muir's entry: "The name 'Wawona Falls' was apparently given by John Muir to one of the many waterfalls among the forks of Big Creek. The exact location of the falls is not known."

The "Telescope Tree" shows axe-marks, interpreted as an aborted effort to tunnel through it, according to: C. A. Harwell, "Mariposa Grove of Big Trees," *Yosemite Nature Notes*, Vol. 10, No. 6, June 1931, p. 52, currently online at yosemite.ca.us/library/yosemite_nature_notes/10/10-6.pdf (accessed 3/21/2023).

The reference to Grant stopping under the "Wah-wah-nah" tree: *San Francisco Chronicle* October 7, 1879. An early (1883) reference to the "Wawona Tree" is found in: N. W. Griswold, *Beauties of California* (1883, H. S. Crocker & Co., San Francisco).

(Gordon and Reynolds 1994) p. 97 makes reference to a ledger that documents the payment of Lyman Scribner for carving the tunnel through the Wawona tree by "enlarging" a pre-existing burn-scar, $198.27 expenses, plus $74 possibly for labor, sometime between 1880 and 1882; the location of the ledger is not cited by the authors. (Sargent, Yosemite's Historic Wawona 1979) p. 35 gives 1881 as the date of the tunneling of the tree (also describing it as the enlargement of a burn-scar), and $75 as the fee paid to the three brothers, Lyman, Otis, and Ben Scribner, but gives no source attribution.

An inventory of named trees in the Mariposa Grove from 1910 mentions a giant sequoia thus: "Hamilton, circumference 85 feet, height 241 feet" somewhere close to the Wawona Tree. If the theory is correct that the original Hamilton Tree had been renamed "Wawona," this would indicate that the Hamilton name was transferred to yet another tree. Unfortunately, documentation of the grove's earlier tree-names remains scant.

See B. M. Leitch, *Mariposa Grove of Big Trees California* (1910, B. M. Leitch).

[162] George Fiske " #376-"Wawona. Showing stage in tree (diameter 30⊚.) Mariposa Grove" J.M. Hutchings is a passenger" (copy negative 1985 by M. Dixon, YM 7051, YOSE Box 66, Yosemite Museum & Archives)

[163] *Mariposa Gazette*, May 31, 1879, pg. 3, col. 3. The reference to the "new constitution" refers to the recent ratification of a newly amended version of the California Constitution.

[164] *Mariposa Gazette*, April 5, 1879, pg. 3, col. 2 and May 31, 1879, pg. 3, col. 2.

[165] Grant arrived in Nagasaki on the 21st of June: (Grant 1885-1886) excerpt from Chronology, pp. 1155–1156.

Article about the band: *Mariposa Gazette*, June 7, 1879, pg. 3, col. 2.

[166] (Grant 1885-1886) excerpt from Chronology, pp. 1155–1156.

[167] *Mariposa Gazette*, July 26, 1879, pg. 2, col. 2, and pg. 3, col. 1. U.S. Census Bureau 1880, San Francisco, CA gives the ages for Frederick and Herbert.

[168] (Grant 1885-1886) excerpt from Chronology, pp. 1155–1156.

Grant's arrival in San Francisco: *Mariposa Gazette*, September 27, 1879, pg. 2, col. 1.

[169] (Kendall 2016)

[170] *Mariposa Gazette*, September 27, 1879, pg. 3, col. 1.

[171] (Remlap 1885) p. 572-578.

[172] Though the report says "dinner," their arrival in Fresno Flats was probably mid-day and the meal would have been, at least in modern terms, lunch. The Grant party had a late dinner that evening at Big Tree Station.

[173] Newspaper quote from: "On To Yosemite," *San Francisco Chronicle*, October 8, 1879.

Regarding anvil firing, see *The Foxfire 40th anniversary book: faith, family, and the land* (Foxfire Fund, Anchor Books 2006), pp. 193–196.

Note: despite the name change to Big Tree Station, news articles often used the more familiar "Clark's" in reference to the hotel.

[174] John F. Miller was a general for the Union in the Civil War, and in 1880 became a California state Senator.

"Col. Dent" refers to Julia Grant's brother, George W. Dent, who came to California in 1852 to mine gold and was later appointed by President Grant as Customs Appraiser in San Francisco (*Los Angeles Herald*, January18, 1899).

[175] Editorial note: "Indigenous people" replaces the pejorative "digger" commonly used at the time.

[176] The *California Great Register* (1892) describes John Eldridge LaTouche as a farmer, born in Massachusetts (1845), 5' 6" tall, light-complexioned with blue eyes and light brown hair —

California Great Registers, 1866-1910, 17 May 1892; citing Voter Registration, Grants Spring, Mariposa, California, United States, county clerk offices, California; FHL microfilm 976,934.

According to his pension record from 1892, LaTouche (aka John E. Phelan) served in L Company of the 19th Mass. Infantry, and K Company of the 4th Mass. Heavy Artillery—*United States General Index to Pension Files, 1861-1934*, Phoebe E LaTouche in entry for John E Latouche Or Phelan, 1892.

An earlier pension record gives LaTouche's rank at discharge as Corporal, under his previous alias Phelan (aka Phelin): *United States Civil War Soldiers Index, 1861-1865*, John E. Phelan, Corporal, Company I, 19th Regiment, Massachusetts Infantry, Union; citing NARA microfilm publication M544 (Washington D.C.: National Archives and Records Administration, n.d.), roll 31; FHL microfilm 881,900.

LaTouche's 19th Mass. Infantry fought in the Battle of the Wilderness under Grant; currently online at: civilwarintheeast.com/us-regiments-batteries/massachusetts/19th-massachusetts (accessed 3/21/2023).

LaTouche's obituary appears in *Mariposa Gazette*, May 20, 1893, pg. 3, col. 6:

"At Twin Springs, Mariposa county, May 16th, 1893, John E. LaTouche, aged 48 years, a native of Massachusetts. The deceased was a pioneer to the mountains of this county, and had many friends among the settlers in his neighborhood. He was an open hearted man, generous to a fault. He served as a private soldier during the civil war, and his record in the army was clear and honorable. A widow and four young children are left free to face the world without him."

177 "Clark's near Big Tree Grove on the Mariposa Trail to Yosemite," by Carleton Watkins (1866 Mammoth Plate No. 105; Neaf and Hult-Lewis No. 976)

178 "The Devil's Nose" refers to Devil Peak, aka Signal Peak, visible from the front of the hotel. There is only one "bed chamber" that would have afforded this view (now obscured by trees) that also links to an adjoining suite of rooms—currently room-number 226—making this a compelling choice for Grant's "bedchamber."

Regarding the article's reference, "At the village and in riding about the region he spent fourteen days," Grant's visit to Yosemite lasted only 7 days.

Grant's reported reference to "Tuolumne" may provide evidence to support the story that Grant had spent time in the vicinity of the Tuolumne and Stanislaus rivers at Knight's Ferry, where in 1852 and 1854 he is said to have visited his wife's brothers (the Dent family). See (Brotherton 1982) p.91; see also "Knight's Ferry Bridge" (HAER CA-314): tile.loc.gov/storage-services/master/pnp/habshaer/ca/ca3100/ca3186/data/ca3186data.pdf (p. 6, footnote 16) accessed 3/19/2022.

179 Catalog # YRL 979.447 Y-40, Yosemite Museum and Archives. Transcription & notes by Tom Bopp [bracketed sections are my additions and interpretation of words].

180 *Mariposa Gazette*, October 4, 1879, pg. 2-3, col. 1.

[181] This photograph was discovered in a collection of images of Yosemite in the possession of the Malone family—onetime residents of Yosemite Valley.

[182] *California Farmer and Journal of Useful Sciences*, Volume 49, Number 21, January 8, 1880 pg. 2 col. 2.

[183] *Mariposa Gazette*, June 14, 1879, pg. 3, col. 1:

> "Yo Semite Chapel Dedicated.—The Yo Semite Chapel, Yo Semite Valley, Mariposa county, was dedicated last Sunday. The dedicatory sermon was preached by Dr. Thomas Guard, of Oakland, and the prayer was made by Rev. Joseph Cook of Boston."

[184] "I never hauled a lady …." quote: (Remlap 1885) p. 576-577, including the reference to Monroe's answering Grant's questions along the way.

[185] (Remlap 1885) p. 576-577.

[186] The *Gazette* corroborates that six horses were used on each of the stages (*Mariposa Gazette*, October 11, 1879, pg. 3, col. 2).

[187] At the time of Grant's visit in 1879, the hotel formerly known as "Clark's Station" and then "Clark & Moore's" was being called "Big Tree Station." On January 12, 1884 the *Gazette* announced the change from Big Tree Station to "Wawona Hotel." Truman's article uses that name in his 1903 article.

[188] Truman's "Jehu" and "Nimshi" are references to the *Old Testament*, 2 Kings 9:20 (King James Version): "And the watchman told, saying, He came even unto them, and cometh not again: and

the driving is like the driving of Jehu the son of Nimshi; for he driveth furiously."

[189] (K. A. Taylor 1926).

[190] *Oakland Tribune, Magazine Section,* March 2, 1924, pg. 7 (Photostat reproduction from California State Library). The illustration, by Pierre N. Boeringer, originally appeared in (Truman, Knights of the Lash: Old Time Stage Drivers of the West Coast March 1898) p. 281-226.

[191] *Mariposa Gazette*, October 4, 1879, pg. 2, col. 1. Of the many spellings of Hiram Lee Rapelje's last name from various sources—newspaper articles, census and marriage records, and the like—"Rapelje" appears to be the most consistent spelling in the kinds of primary records for which Rapelje himself would have personally witnessed.

Reference to the opening of the Madera Road: *Mariposa Gazette,* April 2, 1879, pg. 3, col. 2.

The "ancient driver," Wesley Barton "Billy" Dowst (1829–1885), would have been 50 years old at the time of Grant's visit. Dowst's gravesite in his native Massachusetts gives his birth year and the year his remains were likely moved from Merced to Massachusetts in 1889. His obituary is in: *Mariposa Gazette*, June 27, 1885, pg. 3, col. 2.

"Captain Dowst" quote is from: *Mariposa Gazette*, October 11, 1879, pg. 4, col. 2.

[192] Schlageter's birth is recorded by: *California Death Index, 1940-1997*, Ulrich in entry for Fredrick Wm Schlagater, 30 Nov 1944; Department of Public Health Services, Sacramento.

Quoted account from: Frederick William Schlageter, "General Grant's Visit to Yosemite," Catalog # YRL 979.447 Y-40, Yosemite Museum and Archives. The same document concludes: "Mr. Schlageter is one of the 'old timers' in Mariposa. He was born in San Francisco on October 1, 1859. His father, a blacksmith came to the United States from Germany in 1848 and settled in Louisville, Ky. In 1855 he came to San Francisco. Later the family moved to Mariposa where Mr. Schlageter Sr. worked as a blacksmith for Gallison and Farnsworth for about a year. The family lived in Mariposa until 1846 when they moved to San Francisco. Mr. Schlageter said his family first visited Yosemite in 1874. (The Coulterville Road was just being built and finished that year). They came in over Hite's Cove Trail, this side of Indian Flat, coming into the Merced Canyon at the present site of the Barium Mine, and continuing by trail up the Merced Canyon to Yosemite Valley. (Postmaster F. C. Alexander stated that Mr. Schlageter worked for Mr. Washburn in the post office at Wawona during the summer season for about 25 years). (Nov. 27, 1941)."

[193] (Young 1879) p. 631.

[194] *California Farmer and Journal of Useful Sciences*, Volume 49, Number 21, (January 8, 1880): pg. 2 col. 2.

[195] Many of the various giant sequoias in the Mariposa Grove were given names, a practice that has been mostly abandoned. Addressing the related subject of actually carving one's name onto these trees, along with admonishing that they be left in

"nameless grandeur," the *Gazette* published a poem by a traveler identified as "Walter Bagot, Co. Kildare, Ireland, Big Tree Station" (*Mariposa Gazette*, August 18, 1877 p. 3, col. 3):

"These mighty trees, go stranger, scan;
Study their forms note their span,
But from one custom pray refrain
Of decking these giants with your name,
In nameless grandeur let them stand,
And admiration still command,
When you and I and all our lot
For countless years shall be forgot
Successive young ones take the place,
Of fallen monarchs of the race;
The saplings that you now behold
Three thousand years shall scarce make old."

"Judge Jackson" probably refers to Henry Rootes Jackson, who was a major general in the Confederate States Army during the American Civil War.

The quoted newspaper article is from: *San Francisco Chronicle* October 7, 1879.

[196] (Young 1879) p. 631.

[197] *Mariposa Gazette*, October 11th, 1879 p. 3, col. 2–4.

[198] Newell D. Chamberlain, *The Call of Gold* (1936).

[199] According to the 1880 census, Alexander Pelton was born in 1826 in Alabama and lived in Hornitos with his wife, Lucey, and grandson Thomas Marlin—U. S. Census Bureau (1880),

Alexander Pelton in entry for Lucey Pelton, 1880; citing enumeration district ED 39, sheet 156B, NARA microfilm publication T9 (Washington D.C.: National Archives and Records Administration, n.d), roll 0068; FHL microfilm 1,254,068.

Pelton's 1892 military pension card shows he fought for the Union with the 3rd Regiment Iowa Cavalry, Company L—*United States General Index to Pension Files, 1861-1934*, Alexander Pelton, 1892.

See also currently online: nps.gov/civilwar/search-battle-units-detail.htm?battleUnitCode=UIA0003RC (accessed 3/21/2023).

Pelton died in 1910 and is buried in Saint Catherine's Church Cemetery in Hornitos, CA.

[200] *Mariposa Gazette*, October 11th, 1879 p. 3, col. 2–4, and October 4th, 1879 p. 3, col. 2. Intriguingly, the same article states, "The general was seated on the driver's seat, between Col. Dent and Mr. Dowst the driver, and as soon as he took off his hat he was recognized by the crowd, who cheered him very enthusiastically.

Mr. Lowe had his camera ready, and photographed the party from two different positions. The stage then proceeded to Gallison's Hotel, where the General, after being unearthed from the accumulated dust by the use of a broom administered by Professor Ebony Holman (an African lexiconist of the section) and passing through the usual ablutionary exercise, took a position in the office and shook hands with all those who desired that honor."

So far, no photographs of Grant's visit to Yosemite have surfaced.

[201] *Mariposa Gazette*, May 29, 1880 p. 3, col. 1. On the 1880 U.S. Census Bureau form, San Francisco, CA, for Sarah DeVall, the entry "M" for "Married" is inked out, suggesting that she was recently divorced. Her children, Frederick and Herbert, are listed in her family group (but not Thomas, her former husband), indicating that she did indeed get custody of her sons.

[202] *Mariposa Gazette*, July 17, 1880 p. 3, col. 4.

[203] *Mariposa Gazette*, March 26, 1881, pg. 3, col. 5. Note: the term "instant," abbreviated "inst." meaning "present" or "current" indicates the most recent occurrence of the date referenced in the article

[204] *Pacific Rural Press,* May 7, 1881, pg. 3, col. 2.

[205] *Mariposa Gazette*, August 13, 1881, pg. 3, col. 3.

[206] (Phillips 2001). Ed and John Washburn's return to Big Tree Station reported in a handwritten transcript of *Bellows Falls Times* 9/11/1874 (Wawona Washburn Hartwig Papers, Yosemite Museum and Archives).

[207] "Yosemite Stage and Turnpike Co. Inventory of Stock taken Dec. 31st, 1882" (Washburn Papers, Yosemite Museum and Archives), listing:

Two: Fourteen-Passenger Kimball Wagons $2,000
Three: Eleven-Passenger Kimball Wagons $2,700
Two: Eleven-Passenger Kimball Wagons $1,800
One: Eight-Passenger Kimball Wagon $700
Five: Eleven-Passenger Kimball Wagons $2,000
Four: Eight-Passenger Kimball Wagons $1,025

Two: Five-Passenger Kimball Wagons $600
Two: Buggies $575
Two: Two-seat Spring Wagons $300
Two: Freight Wagons $450
Two: Buckboards $150   Total $12,300
Listed under "Live Stock:"
Eighteen Horses $3,600 [$200 each]
One-hundred fifty-five Horses $15,500 [$100 each]

The Kimball wagons were probably shipped by train from the C. P. Kimball Co. in Chicago. For more on the Kimball company currently online see: carriagemuseumlibrary.org/home/library-archives/carriage-manufacturers/kimballs-of-new-england/ (accessed 3/21/2023).

[208] *Mariposa Gazette*, August 20, 1881, pg. 3, col. 2. Archeological evidence (bedrock mortars, etc.) shows that the Fish Camp area had been inhabited over thousands of years. The 1879 Madera Road opened the area to new settlers employed at mining (at nearby Mt. Raymond), logging, and tourism, prompting construction of hotels, stores, and campgrounds. The name *Fish Camp* may be the alliterative offspring of its neighboring settlement, *Ditch Camp*, two miles away (see *Mariposa Gazette* January 14, 1882, pg. 3 col. 2), probably established to provide housing for the maintenance crew that tended an important utility ditch that diverted water from Big Creek to the Lewis Fork of the Fresno River.

[209] *Mariposa Gazette*, March 11, 1882, pg. 3, col. 2.

[210] Records of Monroe family land acquisitions:

Mariposa Gazette, January 31, 1873, pg. 2, col. 5—Mary Monroe property description 160 acres plus improvements.

Mariposa County, CA—"Index to Federal Land Patents," (accessed online 3/21/2023 at: files.usgwarchives.net/ca/mariposa/land/mariposa.txt)
Meridian MD; Township 0060S; Range 0190E; Section 018; Document I.D. 7157; Date 1880/09/01; Name Lewis A. Monroe.

Mariposa County, CA—"Index to Federal Land Patents," (accessed online 3/21/2023 at: files.usgwarchives.net/ca/mariposa/land/mariposa.txt)
Meridian MD; Township 0060S; Range 0190E; Section 018; Document I.D. 1428; Date 1884/05/15; Name Lewis A. Monroe.

"Delinquent Tax List" *Mariposa Gazette*, January 29, 1881, pg. 2, col. 2
Monroe, George—Possession, interest and claim to pre-emption of S ½ of SE ¼, NW ¼, SE ¼ of SW ¼ section 7, twp 6S, range 19 E. in all 160 acres valued at $200; impts $150; value of personal property $65; total value of all property $415. Total tax $13.07; collector's costs $1.50."

"Delinquent Tax List" *Mariposa Gazette*, February 3, 1883, pg. 4, col. 2
Monroe, George F., Mariposa Road District No. 3.— Possession, interest and claim to pre-emption of S ½ of SE ¼; NW ¼ of SE ¼, SE ¼ of SW ¼, section 7, twp 6S, range 19 E. M D B and M. in all 160 acres valued at $200; impts thereon $150; value of personal property $40; total value of all property $390; total tax $11.78; collector's costs $1.50."

January 9, 1886: Mariposa County, CA—"Index to Federal Land Patents," (accessed online 3/21/2023 at: files.usgwarchives.net/ca/mariposa/land/mariposa.txt) Meridian MD; Township 0060S; Range 0190E; Section 007; Document I.D. 1702; Date 1886/01/09 Name George F. Monroe.

Description of Monroe ranch as 480 acres: *Mariposa Gazette*, December 25, 1886, pg. 3, col. 2; the ad was dated December 11, 1886.

[211] 1866-1898 *Great Register, Mariposa County*, p. 108 (8th Section dated 1884) entry #897: "Millen, George Richard, [age] 57, [born in] Georgia, [occupation] Blacksmith, [residence] Pea Ridge.

An article in *Mariposa Gazette*, July 15, 1882, pg. 3, col. 1, refers to Louis Monroe's barber shop in the past-tense, corroborating Monroe's self-description as "rancher" in the 1880 census.

[212] In the Pea Ridge poem, the line "patched on the butt like a rifle-ball" evidently refers to the practice of "patching" — wrapping rifle balls with cloth or paper before ramrodding them down the rifle bore.

[213] *Mariposa Gazette*, April 16, 1881, pg. 3, col. 2-3.

[214] Earlier articles place the Hambleton operation within two miles of the Monroe Ranch; the quote is from *Mariposa Gazette*, May 22, 1880, pg. 3, col. 3. The reported value of the ore is reported in *Report of the Director of the Mint Upon the Production of the Precious Metals in the United States* (United States. Bureau of the Mint, U.S. Government Printing Office, 1883, currently online at:

books.google.com/books?id=XebOAAAAMAAJ&dq=Hambleton+mine+mariposa&source=gbs_navlinks_s (accessed 3/21/2023).

[215] *Mariposa Gazette*, September 17, 1881, pg. 3, col. 4.

[216] *Mariposa Gazette*, June 24, 1882, pg. 3, col. 2.

[217] (Bailey 1884) pp. 43-44, cited in (Browning 2005) p. 104. Re. inaccuracies in Bailey's remarks, Monroe had indeed been "outside of the State," and had worked well over 12 years for the stage company.

[218] *Mariposa Gazette*, January 12, 1884, pg. 3, col. 1.

[219] The Homestead Act (1862), currently online at: loc.gov/rr/program/bib/ourdocs/homestead.html (accessed 3/21/2023).

[220] *Mariposa Gazette*, May 16, 1885, pg. 3, col. 1.

[221] *Mariposa Gazette*, May 30, 1885, pg. 3, col. 5.

[222] Details of Sullivan's trip recounted: (Hayes 2003).

Images of John L. Sullivan and Sir Arthur Sullivan public domain, shared through: creativecommons.org/licenses/by-sa/3.0/

[223] Article detailing a new road from Madera to Big Tree Station via Grant's Springs, "thirteen miles shorter" than the road via Fresno Flats (Oakhurst), also lauding the work of John Conway who in 1875 engineered the road from Big Tree Station to Yosemite Valley, found in *Mariposa Gazette*, February 6, 1886, pg. 3, col. 1 (see also earlier notes on Conway etc.):

"This piece of road required some good engineering, which was done by Mr. John Conway. Speaking of engineering, such as is necessary to lay off a road similar to this, reminds one that Fisher & Co. paid $1,950 for having the old road surveyed across the mountain from Cold Spring to the Station, while this (by Conway) only cost $50, and the latter was quite as difficult as the former .... A man with an eye to business like John Conway has no use for instruments to survey a road."

[224] Article describing the new railroad depot in Raymond, CA, opening "next Monday" (April 5, 1886): *Mariposa Gazette*, April 3, 1886 p.3, col. 3.

[225] The area occupied by the Monroe Ranch is referred to in the *Mariposa Gazette* alternately as Pea Ridge, Red Mountain, and Chowchilla, the latter referring to its proximity to a branch of the Chowchilla River.

[226] *Mariposa Gazette*, November 27, 1886, pg. 3, col. 4, and November 27, 1886, pg. 3-4, col. 3.

[227] From Truman's 1903 article cited earlier in these notes.

[228] Location of Methodist church: *Mariposa Gazette*, February 12, 1876, pg. 3, col. 2; Murrish's first sermon in Mariposa: *Mariposa Gazette*, October 30, 1886; resigns: *Mariposa Gazette*, September 24, 1887, pg. 3, col. 1. The actual cemetery where Monroe was buried is not specified, but it was reported four years later that Louis Monroe was buried in the "Mariposa graveyard" (*Mariposa Gazette*, May 31, 1890, pg. 3, col. 6), indicating that the Monroes were not excluded on the basis of race, and that the Monroes

preferred the Mariposa cemetery over, for example, burial in the tiny Pea Ridge cemetery. While Gazette articles from the 1880s generally refer to cemeteries by name: "Odd Fellows Cemetery" "Catholic Cemetery" "Masonic Cemetery" and "Public Cemetery," the latter likely indicating the "Mariposa graveyard."

[229] Earliest mention of "Fort Monroe" in my research: "Inventory, Yosemite Stage & Turnpike Co., Dec. 31, 1890" (Washburn Papers, Yosemite Museum and Archives).

Reference to "Freedom's Fortress:" see www.nps.gov/fomr/index.htm; accessed January 2, 2022.

[230] *Mariposa Gazette*, May 23, 1885, pg. 1, col. 6. Article describes the Glacier Point Road: "Beginning at Chinquapin Flat … running in a generally easterly direction through Badger Pass and Monroe Gap and past Peregoy's …."

An online map shows Monroe Meadow as Yosemite's ski area, map currently online at: mapcarta.com/23094000 (accessed 3/21/2023).

[231] *Mariposa Gazette*, December 4, 1886, pg. 3, col. 1.

[232] *Mariposa Gazette*, December 25, 1886, pg. 3, col. 2 (ad dated Dec. 11), and pg. 3, col. 6.

[233] Millen was at Pea Ridge as late as 1886, shown in *1866-1898 Great Register, Mariposa County,* p. 121 (9th Section dated 10/20/1886, entry #889: "Millen, George Richard, [age] 59, [born in] Georgia, [occupation] Blacksmith, [residence] Pea Ridge"). He appears in San Diego in *1887-88 Maxwell's Directory of San Diego City and County* p. 234: "Millen G. R., blacksmith, res 1130 I."

Mary's homestead claim of December 13, 1886 is recounted in documents for the court case "Mary A. Monroe, Plaintiff vs. Wm. G. Grove and D. P. Allen, Defendants," (1887, envelopes 1-3, Mariposa Museum and History Center Collection).

[234] *Mariposa Gazette*, December 25, 1886, pg. 3, col. 2.

[235] Grove obtained judgment against Monroe's ownership on May 24, 1887. Allen's sale of the property was on June 28, 1887.

[236] The record of the case "Mary A. Monroe, Plaintiff vs. Wm. G. Grove and D. P. Allen, Defendants," (1887, envelopes 1-3, Mariposa Museum and History Center). Biographical information about Grove can be found in: *Civil War veterans buried in George C. Yount Pioneer Cemetery in Yountville*, currently online at: freepages.rootsweb.com/~enderlin/history/cw/yountville/yountcem-cwburials.html#grove-wg (accessed 3/21/2023).

[237] *Mariposa Gazette*, April 30, 1910, pg. 4, col. 1; obituary for J. W. Congdon, aged 76.

District Attorney Newman Jones, born in Vermont, continued his career as an attorney in various other cities around California. In Berkeley in September, 1908, he was arrested during a second attempt to break into the home of John M. Corcoran—the judge who had presided over Monroe vs Grove & Allen. Jones reportedly "broke down when questioned by detectives, and said: 'I knew Corcoran kept a flask always in the house. I had to have a drink and having no money thought of entering the house and getting it." Corcoran appears to have helped Jones to recover his career; it was reported by Corcoran's daughter, May, that two months later Jones was employed by the Berkeley law office of

James F. Peck. Jones died in 1941 at the age of 88. See *Los Angeles Herald*, Sep. 27, 1908, *Merced County Sun*, Dec. 11, 1908 (both articles at cdnc.ucr.edu accessed 3/20/2022), and genealogical profile for Lewis Newman Jones at familysearch.org/tree/person/details/L853-QZP. The article covering the break-in attempt misstates Corcoran's name as James H. Corcoran.

[238] Mary's victory in court reported in: *Mariposa Gazette*, May 19, 1888, pg. 3, col. 2.

[239] *Mariposa Gazette*, August 18, 1888, pg. 3, col. 4.

Francis William "Frank" Mello was a Portuguese farmer whose property bordered the Monroe ranch on the west. Charles T. Hoskin ("Old Man Hoskin") was a 77-year-old Englishman who gave his occupation as "miller"—U.S. Census Bureau (1880). His mill was located on the road that would eventually connect the towns of Mormon Bar and Raymond (*Mariposa Gazette*, February 9, 1901)

[240] *Mariposa Gazette*, March 22, 1890, pg. 3, col. 3.

[241] Red Mountain, about two miles south-east of the Monroe ranch, was sometimes used in other *Gazette* articles in lieu of "Pea Ridge" as a name for the general area.

[242] *Mariposa Gazette*, May 31, 1890, pg. 3, col. 6.

[243] *Mariposa Gazette*, September 19, 1891, pg. 2, col. 3.

[244] *Mariposa Gazette*, May 26, 1894, pg. 3, col. 1.

[245] *San Diego Union,* November 16, 1897.

By 1894, the town of Alpine had only begun to transform itself from a tiny stage stop to the beginnings of a town 30 miles east of San Diego. Information currently online at: alpinehistory.org/brief_history_of_alpine.html (accessed 3/21/2023).

[246] For a biographical sketch of Col. John Kastle: (Guinn 1907) p. 548. Also: (Smythe 1907) p. 471.

[247] *San Diego Union,* November 15, 1897.

[248] The descriptions of Mary Monroe's possessions (p. 28), George Millen's and Col. Kastle's comments, Mary's last communications and final days and minutes all come from: (Coroner, City of San Diego 1897).

[249] Data on the Helping Hand Home and Mission currently online at: genealogytrails.com/cal/sdiego/hospitals_inst.htm (accessed 3/21/2023).

[250] *San Diego Union,* November 16, 1897. Mary Monroe had not kept her heritage a secret—in some circles—but she had also not volunteered that information to the Kastles. Discussing his 2011 book about the history of race ambiguity in nineteenth century America, author Daniel J. Sharfstein observed, "There were many stories of people who … were white at work and black at home." For a detailed discussion about the lives of light-complexioned African Americans in the 19th Century, see: Daniel J. Sharfstein, *The Invisible Line: Three American Families and the Secret Journey from Black to White.*

251 *San Diego Union* November 16, 1897.

252 Mount Hope Cemetery Burial Registry, 1868-1909 part 2, pg. 305: "Died November 14; Buried November 16; Mary Monroe; Race: White; Age 75; Sex: Female; Widow; Nativity: America; Where Buried: Lot 11; Row 7; Section 6; Division 5," currently online at: sandiego.gov/digitalarchives/document/burial-registry (accessed 3/21/2023).

253 Mount Hope Cemetery Burial Registry, 1909-1926 part 2, pg. 129: "Died: June 18,
1912; Buried: June 20, 1912; George Millen; Race: Colored; Age 86 years, 10 months, 9 days; Sex: Male; Single; Nativity: Georgia; Where Buried: Lot 39; Row 2; Section 8; Division 6," currently online at: sandiego.gov/digitalarchives/document/burial-registry (accessed 3/21/2023). Not accounting for leap-years, this puts Millen's birth date at August 9, 1825.

Also Death Record of George Millen: *California Death Index, 1905-1939*, George Millen, 1912; citing 18490, Department of Health Services, Vital Statistics Department, Sacramento; FHL microfilm 1,686,046.

254 Yosemite Museum & Archives (Catalog No. YOSE 4497). Identification at the bottom of the photo reads: "Perkins 1217 Polk Street, San Francisco." Alfred Judson Perkins, Sr. (1838–1900) operated his studio at this location from c. 1885–1887 (Kailbourn 2000) pp. 435-436.

BIBLIOGRAPHY

1854-. *Mariposa Gazette.* California: Microfilm at Yosemite Museum and Archives. cdnc.ucr.edu.

1868-1871. *Mariposa Mail.* Angevine Reynolds; microfilm at Yosemite Museum and Archives.

2023. *African Nova Scotians in the Age of Slavery and Abolition, Black Refugees, 1813-1834.* Nova Scotia Archives. Accessed March 7, 2023. novascotia.ca/archives/africanns/results.asp?Search=&SearchList1=4&Language=English.

Alexander, Kathy. 2022. "Legends of Kansas: Cannonball Stage Route." Accessed March 7, 2023. legendsofkansas.com/cannonballstage.html.

1780. *An Act for the Gradual Abolition of Slavery (March 1, 1780).* Yale Law School, The Avalon Project. Accessed March 7, 2023. avalon.law.yale.edu/18th_century/pennst01.asp.

1889. *An Illustrated History of Los Angeles County, California.* Chicago: The Lewis Publishing Co. Accessed March 7, 2023. archive.org/details/illustratedhisto01lewi/page/357.

Bailey, Charles A. 1884. *A Trip to Yosemite and Hetch-Hetchy.* Chas. A. Bailey.

Baldwin, Jr., Samuel C. P. 2015. "Sotterley in Six Parts." Accessed March 7, 2023. baldwinbriscoe.com/the-john-hanson-briscoe-historical-project/.

Baumgartner, Alice L. 2020. *South to Freedom: Runaway Slaves to Mexico and the Road to the Civil War.* Basic Books.

Beasley, Delilah Leontium. 1919. *The Negro Trail Blazers of California.* Times Mirror Printing and Binding House. Accessed March 7, 2023. google.com/books/edition/The_Negro_Trail_Blazers_of_California/Xk8OAQAAIAAJ?hl=en&gbpv=0.

Bennett, Lola. 2002. *Knight's Ferry Bridge.* .S. Department of the Interior; HAER CA-314. Accessed March 7, 2023. tile.loc.gov/storage-services/master/pnp/habshaer/ca/ca3100/ca3186/data/ca3186data.pdf.

n.d. "Black Entrepreneurs in Antebellum America." *The Making of African American Identity, Vol. 1, 1500–1865* (National Humanities Center). Accessed March 7, 2023. nationalhumanitiescenter.org/pds/maai/identity/text4/text4read.htm.

2018. "Black Homesteaders in the Great Plains." Accessed March 7, 2023. news.unl.edu/newsrooms/today/article/black-homesteaders-project-receives-additional-funding.

Brodnax Sr., David. 2007. "Will They Fight? Ask the Enemy: Iowa's African American Regiment in the Civil War." *The Annals of Iowa Vol. 66, No. 3 (Summer 2007)* (State Historical Society of Iowa) 266-292.

Brotherton, Irwin Newton "Jack". 1982. *Annals of Stanislaus County, Volume I "River Towns and Ferries".* Santa Cruz, California: Western Tanager Press.

Browning, Peter. 2005. *Yosemite Place Names: The Historic Background of Geographic Names in Yosemite National Park.* Great West Books.

November 2, 1815. "Census of refugee households settled at the North West Arm of Halifax harbor." Commissioner of Public Records, Nova Scotia Archives. Accessed March 7, 2023. novascotia.ca/archives/africanns/archives.asp?ID=79.

Center for Bibliographic Studies and Research, University of California, Riverside, comp. n.d. "California Digital Newspaper Collection." Riverside, California. Accessed March 7, 2023. cdnc.ucr.edu.

Chamberlain, Newell D. 1936. *The Call of Gold.* Mariposa, California: Gazette Press. Accessed March 7, 2023. yosemite.ca.us/library/call_of_gold.

Chernow, Ron. 2018. *Grant.* Penguin.

2023. *Civil War in California, The.* State of California. Accessed March 7, 2023. parks.ca.gov/?page_id=26775.

Cobb, Thomas Read Rootes. 1851. *A Digest of the Statute Laws of the State of Georgia: In Force Prior to the Session of the General Assembly of 1851.* Christy, Kelsea & Burke. Accessed March 7, 2023. books.google.com/books?id=Tx9FAAAAYAAJ&dq=cobb%20d

igest%20of%20the%20laws%20of%20georgia%201851&pg=P
A828#v=onepage&q&f=false.

Collins, Carvel. 1949. *Sam Ward in the Gold Rush.* Stanford University
Press.

Coroner, City of San Diego. 1897. *Coroner's Inquest No. 524, Nov. 16,
1897.* Inquest, Research Archives, San Diego History Center,
San Diego: Coroner, City of San Diego, filed under: PR 2.69–
F113–2–Coroner #524, Box 15/22.

1995. *Daughters of Republic of Texas - Volume 1.* Paducah, Kentucky:
Turner Publishing Company. Accessed March 7, 2023.
google.com/books/edition/Daughters_of_Republic_of_Texas_Vo
l_I/NzUGjKhemhgC?hl=en&gbpv=0.

Davis-King, Shelly. 1999. "Wawona: What's in a Name? (Comparative
Philology)." Yosemite Museum and Archives.

Finkleman, Paul. 2006, April 6. *Encyclopedia of African American
History, 1619-1895: From the Colonial Period to the Age of
Frederick Douglass.* USA: Oxford University Press. Accessed
March 7, 2023.
books.google.com/books?id=cCMbE4KKlX4C&pg=PA448&lpg
=PA448&dq=1853+washington+d.c.+black+school&source=bl
&ots=xXmOyXZczM&sig=ACfU3U3u4xndLKDkb9bQMf6ZR
7H2OXykBQ&hl=en&sa=X&ved=2ahUKEwjX5OHi1IjiAhUF
DKwKHWxOARYQ6AEwDnoECAgQAQ#v=onepage&q&f=tr
ue.

1998. "Free Blacks in the Antebellum Period." Library of Congress.
Accessed March 7, 2023. loc.gov/exhibits/african-american-
odyssey/free-blacks-in-the-antebellum-period.html.

Gordon, Albert, and Anne Reynolds. 1994. *Stage To Yosemite.* Big Tree
Books.

Grant, Ulysses S. 1885-1886. *Personal Memoirs of U.S. Grant.* New
York: C.L. Webster.

Greenwood, Grace, and Sara Jane aka Lippincott. 1873. *New Life in
New Lands: Notes of Travel.* New York: J. B. Ford & Company.
Accessed March 7, 2023.
books.google.com/books/about/New_Life_in_New_Lands.html?
id=UNjljd978rkC.

Guinn, James Miller. 1907. *A History of California and an Extended
History of Its Southern Coast Counties: Also Containing*

Biographies of Well-known Citizens of the Past and Present, Volume 1. California Historic Record Company.

Hayes, Scott. 2003. *Uncle Arthur: The California Connection.* The Sir Arthur Sullivan Society.

Johnson, Susan Lee. 1999. "Domestic Life in the Diggings—The Southern Mines in the California Gold Rush." In *Over the Edge: Remapping the American West*, edited by Valerie J Matsumoto and Blake Allmendinger, 116-117. University of California Press. Accessed March 7, 2023. publishing.cdlib.org/ucpressebooks/view?docId=ft8g5008gq&chunk.id=d0e3216&toc.depth=1&toc.id=d0e3210&brand=ucpress.

—. 2000. *Roaring Camp: The Social World of the California Gold Rush.* W. W. Norton & Company.

Jordan, Ryan P. 2007. *Slavery and the Meetinghouse: The Quakers and the Abolitionist Dilemma.* Indiana University Press.

Kailbourn, Peter E. Palmquist and Thomas R. 2000. *Pioneer Photographers of the Far West: A Biographical Dictionary, 1840-1865 .* Stanford: Stanford University Press.

Keber, Martha L. 2017. "New Georgia Encyclopedia: French Presence in Georgia." Georgia College and State University. Accessed March 7, 2023. georgiaencyclopedia.org/articles/history-archaeology/french-presence-georgia.

Kendall, Joshua. 2016. *First Dads: Parenting and Politics from George Washington to Barack Obama.* Grand Central Publishing.

Kurutz, Gary. 2005. *Knights of the Lash, The Stagecoach Stories of Major Benjamin C. Truman.* San Francisco: The Book Club of California.

Lapp, Rudolph M. 1977. *Blacks in Gold Rush California.* Yale University Press.

Lester, John Erastus. 1873. *The Yo-Semite, Its History, Its Scenery, Its Development.* Digitized by Dan Anderson, March 2006. Providence, RI: Self Published. Accessed March 7, 2023. yosemite.ca.us/library/lester_yo-semite.html.

Lowe, Gary D, and John Carpenter. 2017. *Clark's Ranch—From Homestead to Big Tree Station.* Stanford Digital Library. Accessed March 7, 2023. stacks.stanford.edu/file/druid:pk391vm0849/Clark%27s%20Ranch-

Galen%20Clark%27s%20Portal%20to%20the%20Mariposa%20
Grove%20of%20Giant%20Sequoia%20%28smaller%20file%29.
pdf.

*Mary A. Monroe, Plaintiff vs. Wm. G. Grove and D. P. Allen,
Defendants.* 1887. Envelopes 1-3, Mariposa Museum and
History Center Collection (Mariposa County Courthouse).

May, Robert E. 1987. "Invisible Men: Blacks and the U.S. Army in the
Mexican War." *The Historian, 49:4* 463-477. Accessed March 7,
2023. latinamericanstudies.org/mex-war/Blacks-Mexican-
War.pdf.

McGrath, Roger. n.d. "California and the Civil War." Accessed March 7,
2023. militarymuseum.org/HistoryCW.html.

Merriam, Clinton Hart. 1979. *Indian Names for Plants and Animals
Among Californian and Other Western North American Tribes.*
Malki-Ballena Press.

Morrison, Michael A. 1997. *Slavery and the American West.* University
of North Carolina Press.

Palmer, Barbara. 2001. "None Darker Than Me: Racial obsession in
19th-century San Diego." *San Diego Weekly Reader.*

Phillips, Thomas Bruce. 2001. "The Bruce's of Mariposa County."
Accessed March 7, 2023. mariposaresearch.net/bruce.html.

Plante, Trevor K. 2001. "Researching African Americans in the U.S.
Army, 1866-1890 - Buffalo Soldiers and Black Infantrymen."
Prologue Magazine Vol. 33, No. 1. Accessed March 21, 2023.
archives.gov/publications/prologue/2001/spring/buffalo-
soldiers.html.

1865. *Proceedings of the California State Convention of Colored
Citizens.* San Francisco: The Elevator. Accessed March 7, 2023.
omeka.coloredconventions.org/files/original/e88f563c343d4026d
d170a2226aa7ead.pdf.

Remlap, L. T. 1885. *The Life of General U. S. Grant.* Park Publishing
Co.

Reynolds, Anne, and Thomas Bruce Phillips. 1999. *Yosemite's
Forgotten Pioneers, The Bruces of Wawona.* Chilnualna Books.

Sargent, Shirley. 1964. *Galen Clark - Yosemite Guardian.* Sierra Club.

—. 1979. *Yosemite's Historic Wawona.* Flying Spur Press.

2009. "Slave to Free," The Making of African American Identity, Vol.
1, 1500–1865." National Humanities Center. Accessed March 7,

2023.
nationalhumanitiescenter.org/pds/maai/identity/text2/text2read.ht
m.

Smith, Stacey L. 2011. "Remaking Slavery in a Free State: Masters and
Slaves in Gold Rush California." *Pacific Historical Review, Vol.
80, No. 1* (University of California Press).

Smythe, William Ellsworth. 1907. *History of San Diego, 1542-1908:
The modern city.* History Co.

1871. *Special Report of the Commissioner of Education on the
Condition and Improvement of Public Schools in the District of
Columbia: Submitted to the Senate June, L868, and to the House,
with Additions, June 13, 1870.* U.S. Government Printing Office.
Accessed March 7, 2023.
books.google.com/books?id=4q4AAAAAYAAJ&pg=PA197&d
q=Resolute+Beneficial+Society+School&hl=en&sa=X&ved=0a
hUKEwjr9MSJg8vfAhUEna0KHUAeCxoQ6AEIMjAC#v=onep
age&q&f=false.

Taylor, Benjamin Franklin. 1878. *Between the Gates.* Chicago: Griggs
& Co.

Taylor, Katherine Ames. 1926. *Lights and Shadows of Yosemite.*
Accessed March 21, 2023.
yosemite.ca.us/library/lights_and_shadows/early_travelers.html.

Taylor, Mrs. H. J. 1936. *Yosemite Indians and Other Sketches.* San
Francisco: Johnck & Seeger. Accessed March 7, 2023.
yosemite.ca.us/library/yosemite_indians_and_other_sketches/gal
en_clark.html.

Thomas, Joe. 2019. *A Synopsis of the History of Moreland Township
and Willow Grove.* Upper Moreland Historical Association.
Accessed March 7, 2023. umha.com/PDFs/Synopis_of_UM.pdf.

Truman, Ben C. March 1898. "Knights of the Lash: Old Time Stage
Drivers of the West Coast." *Overland Monthly, Vol. XXXI* 281-
226.

Truman, Ben C. July 1903. "The Passing of a Sierra Knight." *Overland
Monthly Vol. XLII, No. 1* 33-39.

Turner, Geneva C. 1959. "For Whom Is Your School Named." *Negro
History Bulletin 22, no. 5.* Accessed March 7, 2023.
jstor.org/stable/44215504.

n.d. "United States Census Records." Accessed March 7, 2023. familysearch.org.

2012. *War of 1812 Claimant, St. Mary's County, Maryland, 1828. Biography: John R. Plater (b. 1767 - d. 1832).* Archives of Maryland (Biographical Series). Accessed March 7, 2023. msa.maryland.gov/megafile/msa/speccol/sc5400/sc5496/050600/050630/html/050630bio.html.

2012. *War of 1812 Refugee, St. Mary's County, Maryland, 1814. Biography: Lewis Munroe.* Archives of Maryland (Biographical Series). Accessed March 7, 2023. msa.maryland.gov/megafile/msa/speccol/sc5400/sc5496/051000/051008/html/51008bio.html.

Washburn, Clarence Arthur. n.d. "Diaries, Washburn Papers." Yosemite Museum and Archives.

Wolfe, Linnie Marsh. 1979. *John of the Mountains: The Unpublished Journals of John Muir.* Madison: University of Wisconsin Press.

Woodson, Carter Godwin. 1919. *The Education of the Negro Prior to 1861.* Washington, D. C.: The Associated Publishers, Inc.

Woodson, Carter Godwin, and Rayford Whittingham Logan, . 1918. *The Journal of Negro History.* Association for the Study of Negro Life and History. Accessed March 7, 2023. google.com/books/edition/The_Journal_of_Negro_History/z7aMIZXgDMkC?hl=en&gbpv=0.

Young, John Russell. 1879. *Around the World with General Grant.* New York: The American News Company.

Zelinsky, Wilbur. 1950. *The Population Geography of the Free Negro in Ante-Bellum America, Population Studies, Vol. 3, No. 4.* Population Investigation Committee. Accessed March 21, 2023. latinamericanstudies.org/slavery/Antebellum-Free-Blacks.pdf.

INDEX

Mary A. (Millen), 9, 11, 28, 78, 152, 167, 172, 178
  death of, 175
Monroe Gap, 164
Monroe Meadow, 164
Monroe Ranch, 78, 82, 149, 155, 165, 166
  Fire, 169
  Foreclosure, 172
Moore, Edwin, 91
Mount Hope Cemetery (San Diego), 182, 183
Muir, John, 74
Munroe
  Household, 17
  Lewis Sr. and Jr. (escape to Nova Scotia), 17
Murrish, Rev. J. T., 163

N

Nicaragua, 31
Nova Scotia, 16

P

Paint your wagons (advertisement), 80
Panama, 30
Partida, Stephen ("General"?), 68, 97, 222
Pea Ridge, 2, 78, 149
Pelton, Alexander, 77, 144, 249
Phelan, John E.. *See* LaTouche, John Eldridge
Photographer of Grant party in Mariposa. *See* Lowe, Mr.
Plater, John Rousby, 16

Pre-emption claims. *See* Homestead and pre-emption claims
Property. *See* Homestead and pre-emption claims
Purdy, J. H., 47

R

Railroad, 74, 80, 157
Rapelje, Hiram, 122, 137
Reynolds, Angevine, 166
Ridgway, James, 68, 75
Roads, 74, 88, 91, 93, 113, 114, 224
Rodgers, Moses Logan, 45, 50, 54, 148
Rogers, J. D., 177

S

Samuel & Zenas Fisher & Co., 74, 88, 157
San Diego Coroner's Inquest No. 524, 198
San Diego Electric Railway Company, 177
San Diego, California, xiv, 166, 172
Sanford, Allen, 47
Sargent, Shirley, 211, 226, 235, 238, 241
Schlageter
  Fredrik William, 138
  Herman, 60, 68
Seale, Benjamin, 18
Sell Jr., William Martin, 211
Severn, HMS, 16
Shelly, Joseph, 100, 110, 145
Shoup, Simon, 228
Sidesaddles, 86
Signal Peak. *See* Devil's Nose

ACKNOWLEDGMENTS

This book would not have been possible without the groundbreaking work of the late Mrs. Wawona Washburn Hartwig. She devoted years to organizing and indexing the Washburn Papers in the Yosemite Museum and Archives National Park Service Library (formerly the Yosemite Research Library - YRL). Having lived the final years of the family dynasty in Yosemite, Mrs. Hartwig brought a unique insight into the materials.

I received immeasurable help at the Yosemite Research Library from former NPS Librarians Linda Eade and James Snyder, and more recently Paul Rogers, Ephriam Dickson, and Shelton Johnson. Thanks to the San Diego History Center for bringing to light key sources of the Monroe story, and to the well-organized and helpful staff of the Mariposa Museum & History Center.

Thanks to my friends who offered invaluable help and advice, especially Dorothy Korber and Dennis Kruska. Thanks to Dallas & Ann Calais for supporting my research over many years. Thanks to John Carpenter, Jeff Henderson, and Patty Malone for sharing historic images.

Special thanks to John Oliver Wilson, who has championed my efforts, and through his encouragement and spot-on advice has inspired the improvement and completion of this history.

Above all, my deepest acknowledgment goes to my wife, Diane Detrick Bopp, for her expert insights, guidance, encouragement, and countless hours in the development, design, and refining of this book.

Two Sequoias, One Trunk 1994 by Diane Detrick Bopp

AUTHOR PAGE

Musician/Historian Tom Bopp has entertained and educated Yosemite's guests at the Wawona Hotel and The Ahwahnee since 1983. His interest in Yosemite's cultural history led him to develop interpretive events for the Yosemite National Park Centennial in 1990, the Camp Curry Centennial in 1999, The Ahwahnee 75th Anniversary (2002), Yosemite Heritage Holidays (2003-2009), regular programs on Wawona history, Theodore Roosevelt and John Muir's 1903 camping trip to Yosemite, Yosemite music and culture, and a film documentary called Vintage Songs of Yosemite.

Born in Southern California (1957), Tom studied classical piano for ten years, earning a Bachelor of Arts degree in Music Composition and Theory from UCLA in 1981. He was one of seven out of 40,000 worldwide employees to receive Delaware North Corporation's Legacy Award of Service Excellence in 2006. In 2008, Tom received the annual Yosemite Fund Award (now the Yosemite Conservancy) "in recognition of the significant effort he has made to enhance the value of Yosemite National Park as a national treasure."

READER'S NOTES

Made in the USA
Columbia, SC
30 August 2024

5ffde09f-9b80-4085-836c-3bae370c3f6bR01